Sadlier PHONICS Reading

Level A

Lesley Mandel Morrow
Senior Author

Jane M. Carr   Emily A. Faubion   Joanne M. McCarty

Margaret M. McCullough   Lisa P. Piccinino   Diane M. Richner   Patricia Scanlon

Monica T. Sicilia   Geraldine M. Timlin   Anne F. Windle

Program Consultants

Grace R. Cavanagh, Ed.D.
Principal, P.S. 176
Board of Education
New York, New York

Ann S. Wright
Reading Consultant
Bridgeport Public Schools
Bridgeport, Connecticut

Maria T. Driend
Reading Consultant
Cooperative Educational Services
Trumbull, Connecticut

Eydee Schultz
Staff Development Specialist
Independent Consultant
Springfield, Illinois

Melanie R. Kuhn, Ph.D.
Assistant Professor of Literacy
Rutgers University
New Brunswick, New Jersey

Maggie Pagan, Ed.S.
College of Education, ESOL Specialist
University of Central Florida
Orlando, Florida

Eleanor M. Vargas, M.A.
Resource Specialist Teacher
Los Angeles Unified School District
Los Angeles, California

Frances E. Horton
Supervisor, Title I
Cabell County Public Schools
Huntington, West Virginia

Sharon L. Suskin, M.A.
Assessment Specialist
South Brunswick Public Schools
South Brunswick, New Jersey

Donna A. Shadle
Principal
St. Mary Elementary and Preschool
Massillon, Ohio

Helen Wood Turner, Ed.D.
Deputy Director of Education
Associates for Renewal in Education
Washington, D.C.

Deborah A. Scigliano, Ed.D.
First Grade Teacher
Assumption School
Pittsburgh, Pennsylvania

Sadlier-Oxford
A Division of William H. Sadlier, Inc.

Advisors

The publisher wishes to thank the following teachers and administrators who read portions of the series prior to publication for their comments and suggestions.

Margarite K. Beniaris
Assistant Principal
Chicago, Illinois

Jean Feldman
Consultant, NCEE
Brooklyn, New York

Mary Lee Gedwill
Second Grade Teacher
North Ridgeville, Ohio

Sr. Paul Mary Janssens, O.P.
Principal
Springfield, Illinois

Sr. Francis Helen Murphy, I.H.M.
Editorial Advisor
Philadelphia, Pennsylvania

Pedro Rodriguez
First Grade Teacher
Los Angeles, California

Kathleen Cleary
First Grade Teacher
Warminster, PA

Deborah Gangstad
First Grade Teacher
Carmel, Indiana

Ana Gomez
Second Grade Teacher
Kenner, Louisiana

Stephanie Wilson
Second Grade Teacher
Knightstown, Indiana

JoAnn C. Nurdjaja
Staff Developer
Brooklyn, New York

Dawn M. Trocchio
Kindergarten Teacher
Brooklyn, New York

Noelle Deinken
Kindergarten Teacher
Thousand Oaks, California

Angela Gaudioso
First Grade Teacher
Brooklyn, New York

Patricia McNamee
Principal
Orlando, Florida

Melissa Mannetta
First Grade Teacher
Brooklyn, New York

Mary Jo Pierantozzi
Educational Consultant
Philadelphia, Pennsylvania

Rosemarie Valente
Second Grade Teacher
Newark, New Jersey

Susan Dunlap
Second Grade Teacher
Noblesville, Indiana

Sr. Dawn Gear, G.N.S.H.
Principal
Atlanta, Georgia

Laura A. Holzheimer
L.A. Resource Teacher, Title I
Cleveland, Ohio

Adelaide Hanna
Reading Resource Teacher
Brooklyn, New York

Antoinette Plewa
Principal
North Plainfield, New Jersey

Earl T. Wiggins
Program Specialist, Title I
Lehigh, Florida

Acknowledgments

Special thanks to Sr. Irene Loretta, IHM, for her advice and counsel during the early developmental stages of the *Sadlier Phonics* program.

William H. Sadlier, Inc., gratefully acknowledges the following for the use of copyrighted materials:

"Good Books, Good Times!" (text only), copyright © 1985 by Lee Bennett Hopkins. Appears in GOOD BOOKS, GOOD TIMES!, published by HarperCollins Publishers. Reprinted by permission of Curtis Brown, Ltd.

"Parades" (text only) from MY DADDY IS A COOL DUDE AND OTHER POEMS by Karama Fufuka. Copyright © 1975 by Karama Fufuka. Used by permission of Dial Books for Young Readers, a division of Penguin Putnam Inc.

"Bugs" (text only) is from *The Fish with the Deep Sea Smile* by Margaret Wise Brown, © 1966 by Roberta Rauch. Reprinted by permission of Linnet Books/The Shoe String Press, Inc., North Haven, Connecticut.

"Yesterday's Paper" (text only) by Mabel Watts. Reprinted with permission of Patricia Watts Babcock, who controls all rights.

"Ears Hear" (text only) by Lucia and James Hymes, Jr., from OODLES OF NOODLES, © 1964 by Lucia and James Hymes, Jr. Reprinted by permission of Addison Wesley Longman.

"Clouds" (text only) by Christina G. Rossetti.

"Tommy" (text only) by Gwendolyn Brooks, copyright © 1956 by Gwendolyn Brooks Blakely. Used by permission of HarperCollins Publishers.

ZB Font Method Copyright © 1996 Zaner-Bloser

Product Development and Management

Leslie A. Baranowski

Photo Credits

Harold Taylor Abipp: 327 *bottom right*; Diane Ali: 299 *top, background*, 331 *panel 6 top right*, 332 *left, panel 2 background, panel 5 center, bottom*, 333 *top left*; Animals/Animals, David Barnes: 315 *top right*, 336 *top right*; George Bernard: 153 *top right*; Stephen Dalton: 153 *top left*; Breck P. Kent: 161 *top, bottom left*, 331 *panel 3 top right*, 335 *bottom right*, 336 *top right*. James Balog: 327 *top right*; Myrleen Cate: 54 *top left*; Cate Photography: 299 *left*; E.R. Degginger: 328 *top right*; Earth Scenes, E.R. Degginger: 332 *panel 7*; Donald Specker: 331 *panel 6 center*. ENP Images, Gerry Ellis: 336 *bottom left*; Neal Farris: 243, 244; Kathy Ferguson: 331 *panel 3 top right*; Michael Fogden: 161 *right*; Zefa Hahn: 315 *center right*; Ken Karp: 11, 162, 245 *bottom right*, 258, 280, 300, 316; Richard Kolar: 327 *bottom left*; Ross Harrison Koty: 331 *top center, left*; John Lemker: 299 *bottom right*; Renee Lynn: 331 *panel 6 bottom*; Raymond Mendez: 327 *top left*; Frank Moscati: 315 *center top*; Natural Selection, Steven M. Rollman: 153 *bottom right*, 154 *bottom right, bottom left*; Jose Pelaez: 315 *bottom center*; Frances Roberts: 81 *bottom right*; H. Armstrong Roberts: 279 *top right, center right, bottom*, 315 *bottom left, center*, 328 *bottom left*, 332 *panel 4 top, panel 2 top, bottom, panel 5 top*, 333 *bottom right*, 334 *left*; J.H. Robinson: 328 *top left*; Kevin Schaefer: 315 *bottom right*; The Stock Market, Nadine Markova: 154 *top right*; Tony Stone Images: 315 *top left*; Stephen Studd: 333 *top right*; Chuck Savage: 279 *left*; A & J Verkaik: 299 *center right*; Steve Vidler/Nawrocki Stock Photography: 81 *top, bottom left*; Visuals Unlimited, Bill Beatty: 335 *top right*; John Gerlach: 335 *top left*; William S. Ormerod, Jr.: 153 *bottom left*; Dick Poe: 335 *bottom left*, 336 *top left*; Richard Walters: 336 *bottom right*. John Warden: 328 *bottom right*; Ralph Wetmore II: 334 *right*; David Young Wolff: 331 *top left*.

Illustrators

Dirk Wunderlich: Cover

Bernard Adnet: 17; JoLynn Alcorn: 93, 106, 233; Shirley Beckes: 79, 90; Linda Bild: 43; Paige Billin-Frye: 223, 252, 266, 283; Lisa Blackshear: 162; Nan Brooks: 293; Jenny Campbell: 45, 89, 95, 105, 122, 140, 230, 246, 248, 254, 261; Terri & Joe Chicko: 13, 81, 220, 271; Bruce Day: 118, 136, 152; Denise & Fernando: 41, 53; Rob Dunlavey: 29, 39, 47, 305; Jim Durk: 103, 104, 249; Cameron Eagle: 35, 40, 65; Dagmar Fehlau: 25; Rusty Fletcher: 19, 186, 263; Arthur Friedman: 323, 324; Barbara Friedman: 109, 121, 277; Dave Garbot: 130, 181; Adam Gordon: 327, 328; Myron Grossman: 239, 296; Tim Haggerty: 59, 280; Susan Hall: 155; Laurie Hamilton: 124, 156; John Stephen Henry: 196, 274; Tim Huhn: 87, 88; Ann Iosa: 314; Megan Jeffrey: 179, 195, 221; Dave Jonason: 31, 96; Karol Kaminski: 7, 27, 51, 74, 300, 316; Andy Levine: 58, 63, 168, 187, 204, 212, 221, 226, 234, 278, 295, 308; Jason Levinson: 82, 83, 86, 101, 127, 159, 160, 183, 188, 199; Judy Dufour Love: 119, 120, 285; Ben Mahan: 61; Maria Pia Marrella: 257; Christine Mau: 258; Patrick Merewether: 143; Judy Moffatt: 209, 210, 312; John Nez: 325, 326; Olivia: 115, 310; Leah Palmer Preiss: 5; Mick Reid: 311; Bart Rivers: 291; BB Sams: 55; Alfred Schrier: 137, 138, 167; Stacey Schuett: 303, 329, 330; Clive Scruton: 287; Teri Sloat: 307; Jamie Smith: 15, 71, 165, 227, 228, 275, 289; Jackie Snider: 30, 37, 66; Sally Springer: 180, 203, 211, 229, 245, 270; Matt Straub: 192, 193, 194; Steve Sullivan: 6, 14, 84, 166, 262, 284, 304; Don Tate: 91, 108, 142, 253, 281, 313; Terry Taylor: 23; Neecy Twinem: 62, 267; Sally Vitsky: 48; Susan Williams: 290; Eddie Young: 177, 178; Jerry Zimmerman: 129, 139. Functional Art: Diane Ali, Sommer Keller, and Michael Woo.

ISBN: 0-8215-7001-3
456789/04 03 02

Contents

Punchout Letter and Picture Cards

**Helpful Hints: Phonics Definitions
and Rules** (See inside back cover.)

GOOD BOOKS, GOOD TIMES!

Good books.
Good times.
Good stories.
Good rhymes.

Good beginnings.
Good ends.
Good people.
Good friends.

Good fiction.
Good facts.
Good adventures.
Good acts.

Good stories.
Good rhymes.
Good books.
Good times.

Lee Bennett Hopkins

Critical Thinking

Why do you like some books more than others?
Where is the best place to read a book?

LESSON 1: Phonemic Awareness and Auditory Discrimination
Phonemic Awareness: Rhyme

Name _____

Dear Family,

In this unit, your child will be listening for words that rhyme or begin with the same sound. He or she will be talking about the fun of reading books. You can enjoy this unit with your child by trying these activities at home.

• Read the poem "Good Books, Good Times!" on the reverse side of this page as your child follows along.

Apreciada Familia:

En esta unidad se enseñarán palabras que riman o que empiezan con el mismo sonido. Los niños estarán hablando de lo divertido que es leer libros. Ustedes pueden disfrutar junto al niño de esta unidad haciendo esta actividad juntos en la casa.

• Lean, en voz alta, el poema en la página 5 mientras su hijo lo repite.

• Ask your child to listen as you read the poem aloud again. Name pairs of rhyming words together. (**times/rhymes, ends/friends, facts/acts**)

• Talk about a favorite book you have read together.

• Visit your local library and find a new book to share.

• Pidan al niño que escuche el poema mientras se le lee en voz alta otra vez. Nombren pares de palabras que rimen. (**times/rhymes, ends/friends, facts/acts**)

• Hablen del libro que leyeron juntos y que les gustó.

• Visiten la biblioteca del vecindario y busquen un libro que puedan compartir.

PROJECT

Have fun with beginning sounds. Say a word like **book** and ask your child to say another word that begins with the same sound, such as **bike**. Take turns thinking of words.

PROYECTO

Diviértanse con los sonidos. Diga una palabra, por ejemplo **book** y pida al niño decir otra que empiece con el mismo sonido, tal como **bike**. Túrnense para pensar en las palabras.

Book and **cook** are rhyming words.
Listen for these rhyming words.

Dad reads the book.
I get to cook!

Name the first picture in each row. Then circle the pictures that have rhyming names.

LESSON 2: Discriminating Rhyming Sounds
Phonemic Awareness: Rhyme

Say the name of each picture. Draw lines to connect the pictures that have rhyming names.

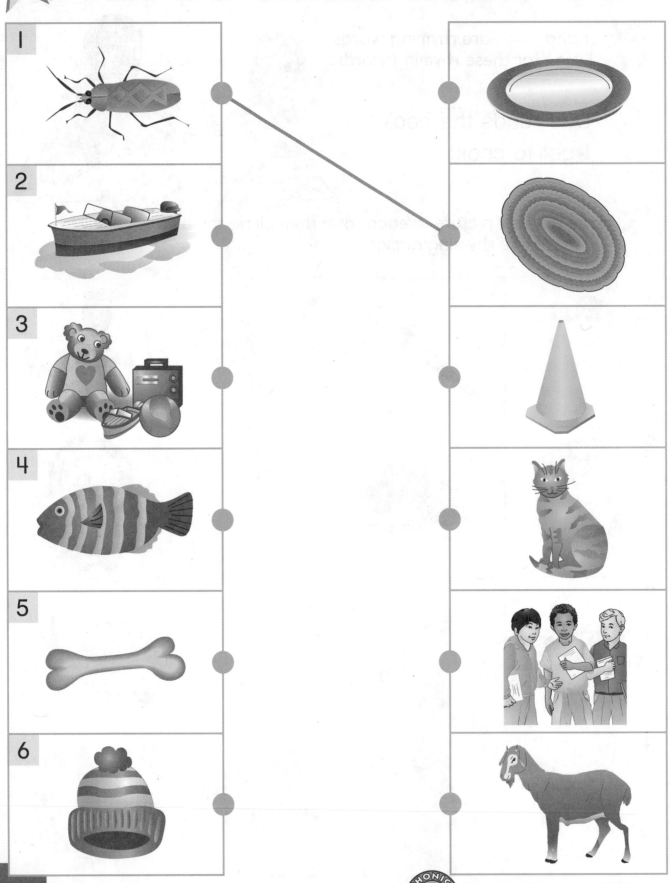

LESSON 2: Discriminating Rhyming Sounds
Phonemic Awareness: Rhyme

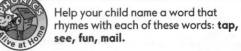

Help your child name a word that rhymes with each of these words: **tap, see, fun, mail.**

Book and **box** have the same beginning sound. Circle and color the picture if its name has the same beginning sound as the first picture in the row.

LESSON 3: Discriminating Initial Sounds
Phonemic Awareness: Initial Sounds

9

Say the names of the pictures on each book. If their names begin with the same sound, circle the book.

1.

2.

3.

4.

5.

6.

7.

8.

LESSON 3: Discriminating Initial Sounds
Phonemic Awareness: Initial Sounds

Say three words, two of which begin with the same sound. Have your child name the two words that begin alike.

Look and Learn

Listen as the page is read aloud. Look at the pictures. Then talk about what you see.

Look at a good book.
Books are stories written down.
Some books tell made-up stories.
Some books tell true stories.
It's fun to read books, and
it's fun to write them, too.

What stories do books tell?

RAIN FOREST

LESSON 4: Phonemic Awareness and Auditory Discrimination in Context
Comprehension: Recalling Details

Check-Up

Circle and color the picture if its name has the same beginning sound as the first picture in the row.

LESSON 4: Assessing Initial Sounds

Review this Check-Up with your child.

Read Aloud

PARADES

I like to see parades
with the marching bands
and big bass drums;
They make me want to dance
and clap my hands.

People ride in convertible cars
and smile and wave at you
and clowns come down the street
and make you laugh.

A parade makes everybody happy;
people talk and dance and sing—
I like to watch parades
more than any other thing.

Karama Fufuka

Critical Thinking

Why do people have parades?
What other kinds of celebrations are fun?

LESSON 5: Consonant Sounds
Phonemic Awareness: Rhyme

13

Dear Family,

In this unit about celebrations, your child will learn the sounds of the consonant letters. As your child progresses through this unit, you may wish to try these activities together at home.

• The consonant letters of the alphabet are shown below. Help your child find the consonants in his or her name.

Apreciada Familia:

Esta unidad es sobre las celebraciones. Los niños aprenderán el sonido de las consonantes. A medida que se avanza en la unidad, pueden hacer estas actividades con su hijo.

• Las consonantes son mostradas abajo. Ayude al niño a encontrar las consonantes en su nombre.

• Read the poem "Parades" on the reverse side of this page.

• Help your child identify some of the consonants in the poem.

• With your child, think of words that rhyme with **band** and **sing**. (hand/land/sand, bing/ding/king/ping/ring/wing)

• Lea el poema "Parades" en la página 13.

• Ayude al niño a identificar las consonantes en el poema.

• Junto con su niño piensen en palabras que rimen con **band** y **sing**. (hand/land/sand, bing/ding/king/ping/ring/wing)

PROJECT

What kinds of celebrations are special for your family? Look at a calendar together and mark the dates of a few of them. Talk about why these days are important. How does your family celebrate them? Help your child find and name some consonants in the names of these celebrations.

PROYECTO

¿Cuáles celebraciones son especiales en su familia? Juntos busquen en un calendario las fechas de algunas. Hablen sobre esos días importantes. ¿Cómo celebra la familia esos días? Ayude al niño a encontrar algunas consonantes en los nombres de esas celebraciones.

Circle the pictures if their names have the same ending sound as the first picture or pictures in the box.

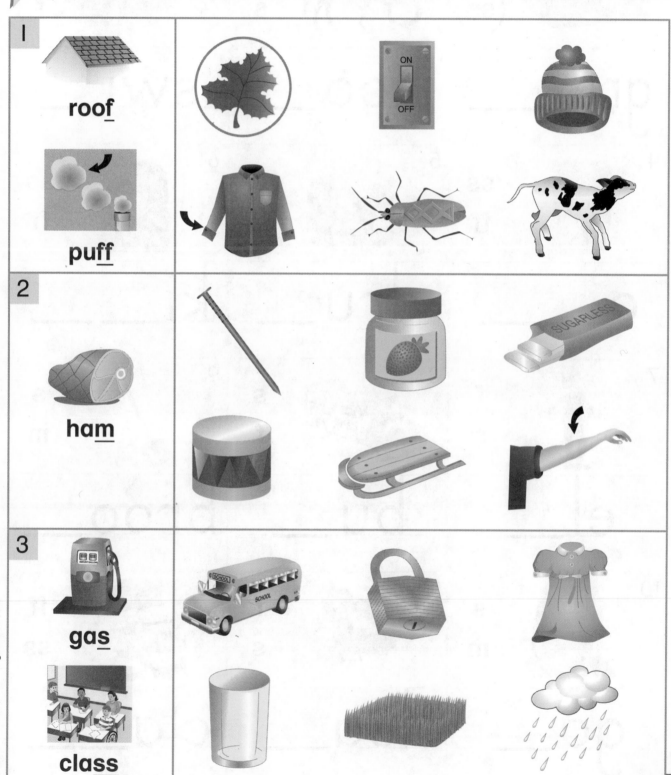

1 | roof | puff

2 | ham

3 | gas | class

Say the name of each picture. Circle the letter or letters that stand for its ending sound. Then print the letter or letters on the line.

1 ff **ss** ⃝ gra___	**2** f s hoo___	**3** m f swi___
4 ss ff o___	**5** s m dru___	**6** ss ff ki___
7 f s el___	**8** s f bu___	**9** s m broo___
10 s m ga___	**11** f s lea___	**12** ff ss cla___

LESSON 9: Connecting Sound to Symbol:
Final /f/ **f, ff;** /m/ **m;** /s/ **s, ss**

PHONICS
Alive at Home

Help your child cut out the pictures.
Sort them into groups that end with
the sound of **f, m,** and **s.**

Tt

Ten starts with the sound of **t**. Listen for the sound of **t** in the rhyme.

Today is my birthday.
It's Tammy's birthday, too.
Today we turn ten.
How old are you?

Circle and color each picture that has the sound of **t** at the beginning of its name.

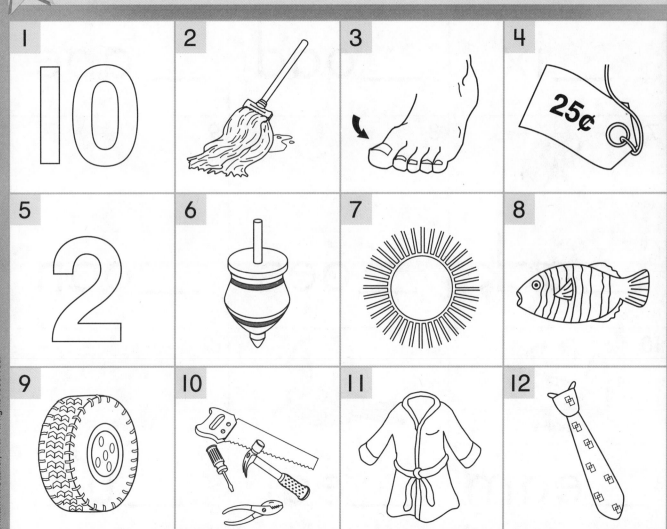

1	2
3	4
5	6
7	8
9	10
11	12

1 __oys	2 __ork	3 __ail
4 __ix	5 __oad	6 __ape
7 __ack	8 __oes	9 __oon
10 __eam	11 __eal	12 __ub

LESSON 10: Connecting Sound to Symbol: Initial /t/ t

Help your child find things in your home that have names beginning with the **t** sound. Set them on a table.

Hh

Horn starts with the sound of **h**. Listen for the sound of **h** in the rhyme.

Honk your horn
And shout, "Hooray!"
Have a happy holiday.

Circle and color each picture that has the sound of **h** at the beginning of its name.

LESSON 11: Phonemic Awareness: Initial /h/

25

1 __at	2 __am	3 __ut
4 __itt	5 __and	6 __op
7 __eel	8 __ay	9 __eed
10 __ose	11 __ape	12 __ot

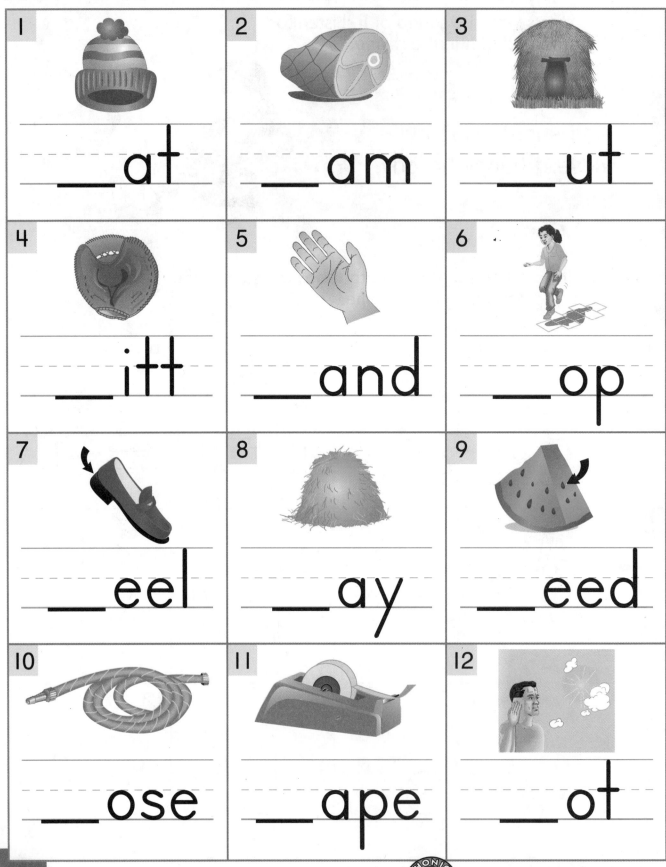

26

LESSON 11: Connecting Sound to Symbol: Initial /h/ **h**

Randomly point to a picture. Have your child give you a high five if its name begins with the sound of **h.**

Bat and **Matt** end with the sound of **t**. Circle the picture if its name has the same ending sound.

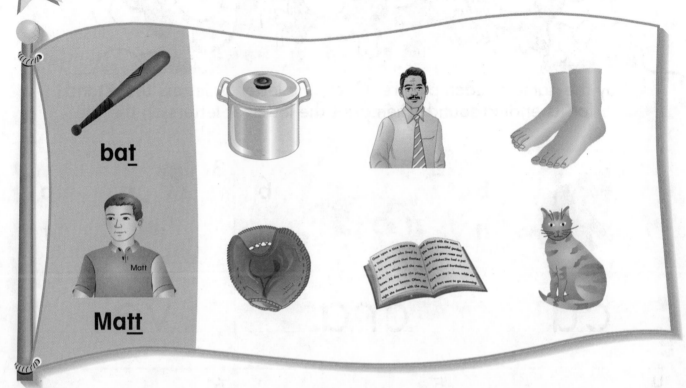

Tub ends with the sound of **b**. Circle the picture if its name has the same ending sound.

LESSON 13: Phonemic Awareness: Final /t/ and /b/   **29**

Say the name of each picture. Circle the letter or letters that stand for its ending sound. Then print the letter or letters on the line.

1 b tt **cu**	2 b tt **cra**	3 b t **ve**
4 t b **ca**	5 tt b **mi**	6 tt b **co**
7 b t **ki**	8 t b **nu**	9 t b **an**

LESSON 13: Connecting Sound to Symbol:
Final /t/ t, tt; /b/ b

With your child, name each object on this page, stressing the end sound: mitt-t-t-t; cub-b-b-b.

Say the name of each picture. Circle the letter that stands for the missing sound. Then print the letter on the line.

1	t s	2	f m	3	h b
__ag		__op		__ed	

4	s m	5	f t	6	h f
__un		__ox		__en	

7	m t	8	b f	9	s t
ja__		lea__		nu__	

10	h s	11	f t	12	b m
bu__		ha__		tu__	

LESSON 14: Reviewing Initial and Final
Consonants f, m, s, t, h, b

31

Check-Up Say the name of each picture. Find the letter in the box that stands for the missing sound. Then print the letter on the line.

f	m	s	t	h	b

1	2	3
__op	__an	__ug

4	5	6
__ap	__op	__ix

7	8	9
we__	ba__	ha__

10	11	12
ga__	roo__	ne__

LESSON 14: Assessing Initial and Final
Consonants **f, m, s, t, h, b**

Review this Check-Up with your child.

Lunch starts with the sound of **l**. Listen
for the sound of **l** in the rhyme.

Lunch, lunch, lunch,
There's lots to eat.
Let's sit by the lake
And munch, munch, munch.

Circle and color each picture that has the sound of **l**
at the beginning of its name.

1	2	3	4
5	6	7	8
9	10	11	12

1	2	3
__eg	__amb	__ask

4	5	6
__oys	__ist	__ime

7	8	9
__eash	__eaf	__ive

10	11	12
_____	__un	__id

34

LESSON 15: Connecting Sound to Symbol: Initial /l/ l

Dd

Dance starts with the sound of **d.** Listen for the sound of **d** in the rhyme.

Dance, dance, dance,
Get on your feet.
Dance, dance, dance,
Don't miss a beat.

Circle and color each picture that has the sound of **d** at the beginning of its name.

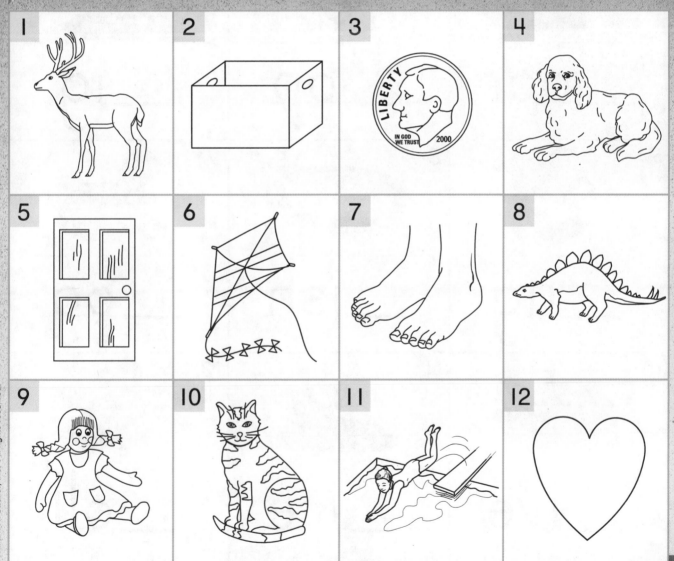

LESSON 16: Phonemic Awareness: Initial /**d**/

35

Say the name of each picture. Print **d** on the line if its name begins with the sound of **d.**

1 __uck	2 __ug	3 __esk
4 __oor	5 __op	6 __ig
7 __ug	8 __ish	9 __og
10 __ive	11 __ire	12 __oll

LESSON 16: Connecting Sound to Symbol: Initial /d/ d

Take turns with your child naming words that begin with the sound of **d.**

Pail and **bell** end with the sound of **l.** Circle the picture if its name has the same ending sound.

pai<u>l</u>

be<u>ll</u>

Bed and **Todd** end with the sound of **d.** Circle the picture if its name has the same ending sound.

be<u>d</u>

To<u>dd</u>

☆ **S**ay the name of each picture. Circle the letter or letters that stand for its ending sound. Then print the letter or letters on the line.

1	ll	2	tt	3	d
	dd		dd		f

be____   a____   sle__

4	ss	5	d	6	m
	ll		l		d

we____   re__   bu__

7	ff	8	l	9	l
	ll		s		d

hi____   mai__   sea__

LESSON 18: Connecting Sound to Symbol:
Final /l/ l, ll; /d/ d, dd

Have your child hold up something red if he or she hears the sound of **d** at the end of these words: **had, bed, will, fill, Todd.**

Ww

Waves starts with the sound of **w**. Listen for the sound of **w** in the rhyme.

Willy wiggles and giggles.
Willy watches and waves.
Willy's next!
Will he be brave?

Circle and color each picture that has the sound of **w** at the beginning of its name.

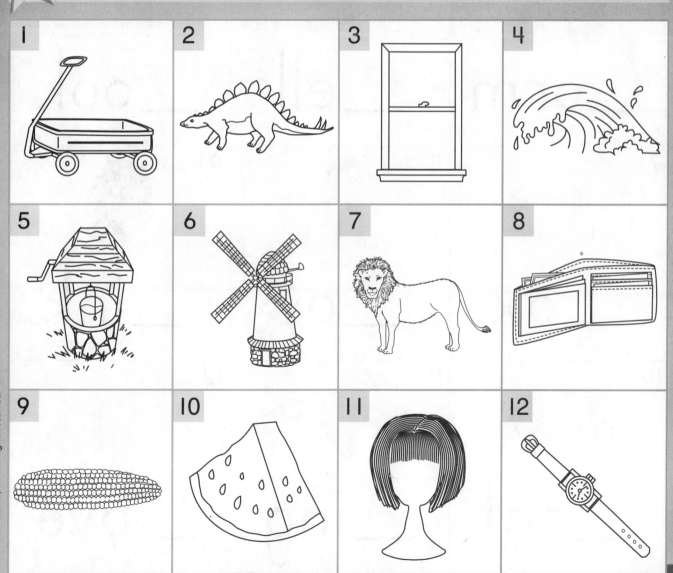

1	2	3	4
5	6	7	8
9	10	11	12

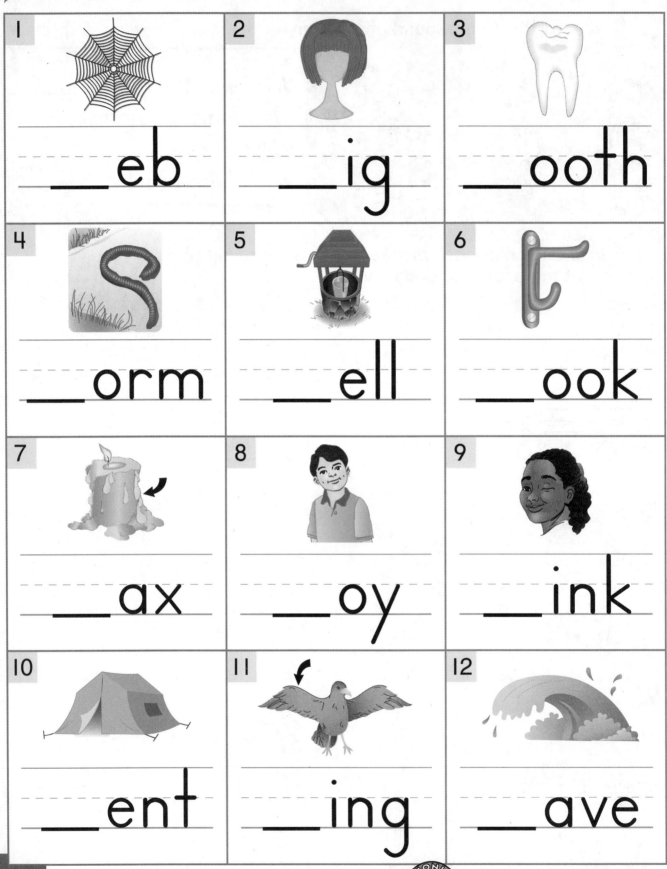

1 __eb

2 __ig

3 __ooth

4 __orm

5 __ell

6 __ook

7 __ax

8 __oy

9 __ink

10 __ent

11 __ing

12 __ave

LESSON 21: Connecting Sound to Symbol: Initial /w/ w

Print **Welcome** on a sheet of paper. Let your child trace the **W** and decorate the sign.

Pan ends with the sound of **n.** Circle the picture if its name has the same ending sound.

pa<u>n</u>

Log and egg end with the sound of **g**. Circle the picture if its name has the same ending sound.

lo<u>g</u>

e<u>gg</u>

Say the name of each picture. Circle the letter or letters that stand for its ending sound. Then print the letter or letters on the line.

1 **n** **s** fa___	2 **ff** **gg** e____	3 **g** **t** do___
4 **g** **n** ru___	5 **d** **n** pe___	6 **g** **n** le___
7 **d** **g** ba___	8 **n** **g** fi___	9 **l** **n** su___

48

LESSON 22: Connecting Sound to Symbol:
Final /n/ n; /g/ g, gg

Take turns reading each word. Have your child name the letter or letters that stand for the ending sound.

Say the name of each picture. Circle the letter that stands for the missing sound. Then print the letter on the line.

1 w n __ose	**2** d l __eaf	**3** g c __ame
4 c n __ake	**5** g w __ink	**6** d n __uck
7 l f mai__	**8** d n sle__	**9** l g do__
10 f n bu__	**11** t l sea__	**12** l d be__

 **Check-Up** Say the name of each picture. Find the letter in the box that stands for the missing sound. Then print the letter on the line.

l	d	c	n	g	w

1	2	3
__ig	__ax	__ut

4	5	6
__og	__at	__um

7	8	9
pi__	ca__	re__

10	11	12
ju__	pai__	te__

LESSON 23: Assessing Initial and Final
Consonants l, d, c, n, g, w

PHONICS Alive at Home   Review this Check-Up with your child.

Pp

Ponies starts with the sound of **p.** Listen for the sound of **p** in the rhyme.

Ponies and poodles
And parakeets, too.
They're having a pet parade
Just for you.

Circle and color each picture that has the sound of **p** at the beginning of its name.

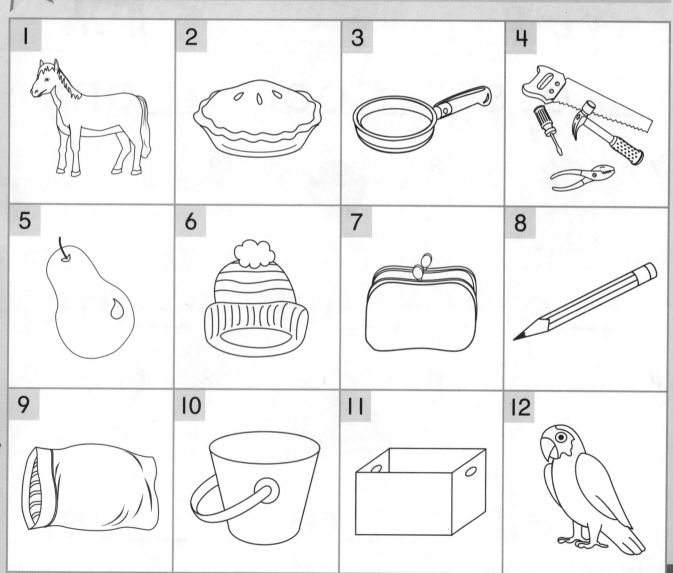

1 2 3 4

5 6 7 8

9 10 11 12

1. ___ot

2. ___oor

3. ___en

4. ___oys

5. ___ool

6. ___ony

7. ___et

8. ___irl

9. ___ink

10. ___ell

11. ___ay

12. ___eel

LESSON 24: Connecting Sound to Symbol: Initial /p/ p

Practice saying this tongue twister together: Peter Piper picked a peck of pickled peppers for Paula's party.

Rr

**R**ed starts with the sound of **r**. Listen for the sound of **r** in the rhyme.

Red rover, red rover,
Let Rosita come over.

Circle the pictures that have the sound of **r** at the beginning of their names.

1. __ing

2. __ope

3. __ish

4. __ule

5. __ock

6. __ed

7. __oad

8. __et

9. __ake

10. __ug

11. __ose

12. __ine

LESSON 25: Connecting Sound to Symbol: Initial /r/ **r**

Say the name of each picture. Have your child repeat any name that begins with the sound of **r**.

Kk

Kettle starts with the sound of **k**. Listen for the sound of **k** in the rhyme.

Katie put the kettle on,
Katie put the kettle on,
Katie put the kettle on,
We'll all have tea.

Circle and color each picture that has the sound of **k** at the beginning of its name.

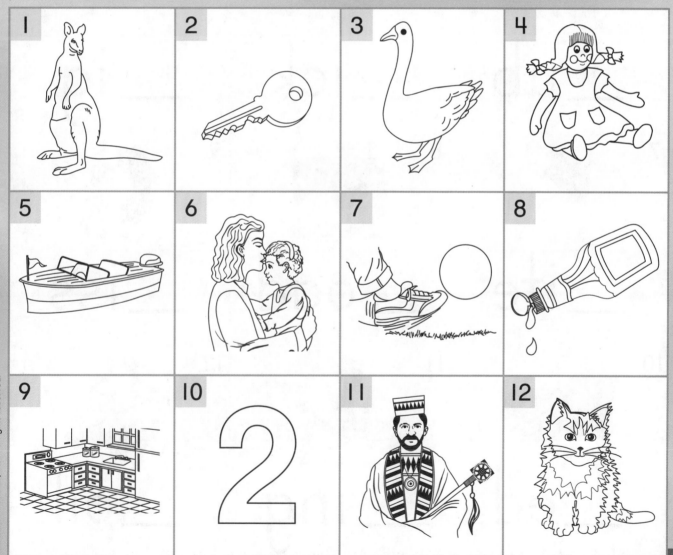

ay the name of each picture. Print **k** on the line if its name begins with the sound of **k.**

1 __ey	2 __ate	3 __it
4 __ub	5 __ick	6 __ig
7 __ite	8 __oad	9 __iss
10 __ed	11 __ing	12 __oll

LESSON 26: Connecting Sound to Symbol: Initial /k/ **k**

Name the pictures. Let your child shake a set of keys after each word that begins with the sound of **k.**

Say the name of each picture. Circle and color the pictures that have the same ending sound as the picture in the box.

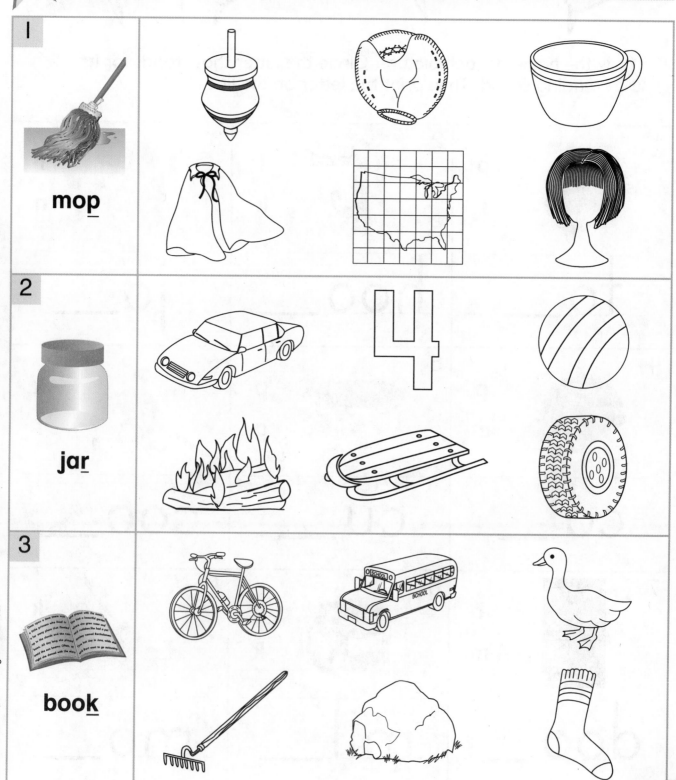

1

mo**p**

2

ja**r**

3

boo**k**

LESSON 27: Phonemic Awareness: Final /p/, /r/, /k/

57

1 p r to___	**2** l k hoo___	**3** r n ja___
4 p m ca___	**5** p g cu___	**6** k f coo___
7 r m doo___	**8** d k mil___	**9** k p mo___

LESSON 27: Connecting Sound to Symbol:
Final /p/ p, /r/ r, /k/ k

PHONICS
Alive at Home

Say the name of each picture. Have
your child clap if its name ends with
the sound of **p**.

Joy starts with the sound of **j**. Listen for the sound of **j** in the rhyme.

Justin and Jasmin
Jump for joy.
The puppy in the jeep
Is theirs to keep.

Circle and color each picture that has the sound of **j** at the beginning of its name.

1	2	3
__et	__ing	__ar

4	5	6
__ug	__eep	__ite

7	8	9
__en	__eans	__acks

10	11	12
__oat	__ed	__am

LESSON 28: Connecting Sound to Symbol: Initial /j/ j

PHONICS Alive at Home

Have your child look at a calendar to find the months with names that begin with the sound of j.

Qu qu

Quiet starts with the sound of **qu.** Listen for the sound of **qu** in the rhyme.

"Shh! Quiet!" said the queen.
"Quick! Hide!" said the king.
Here comes Farmer Green!

Circle the pictures that have the sound of **qu** at the beginning of their names.

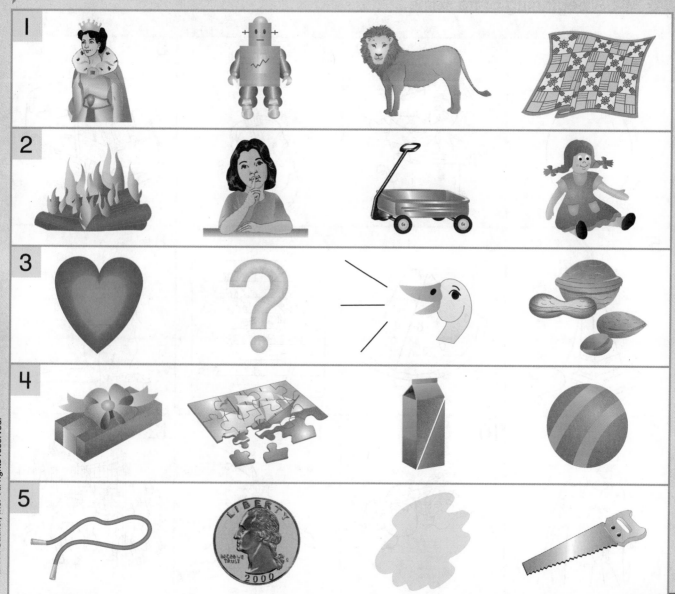

Vase starts with the sound of **v**. Listen for the sound of **v** in the rhyme.

Vv

A big vase of violets
And velvet hearts, too,
Are the Valentine gifts
I'd like to give to you.

Circle and color each picture that has the sound of **v** at the beginning of its name.

1

2

3

4

5

6

7

8

9

10

11

12

LESSON 29: Phonemic Awareness: Initial /v/

Help your child cut out a Valentine heart. Write words that begin with **v** on it.

Say the name of each picture. Color the space brown if the name ends with the sound of **v**. What picture do you see?

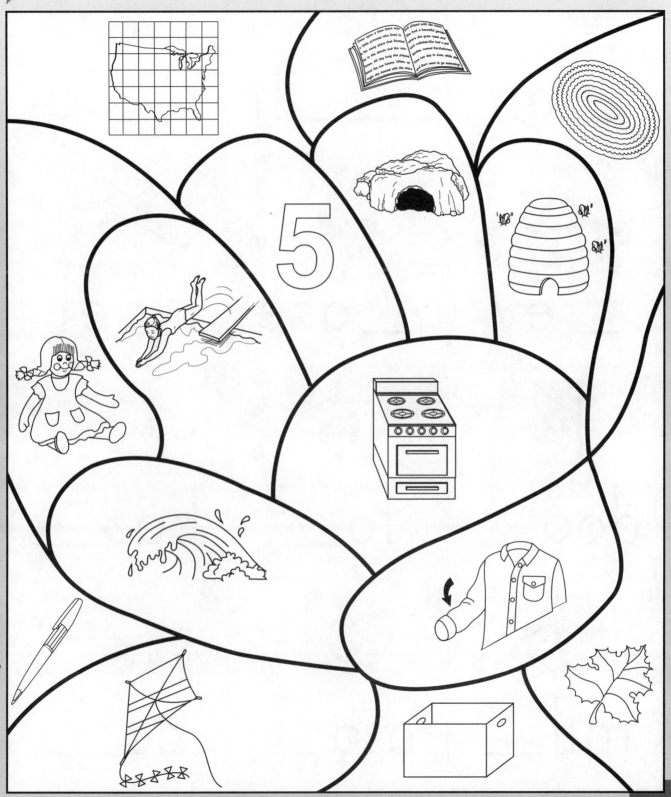

Say the name of each picture. Circle the letter or letters that stand for the missing sound. Then print the letter or letters on the line.

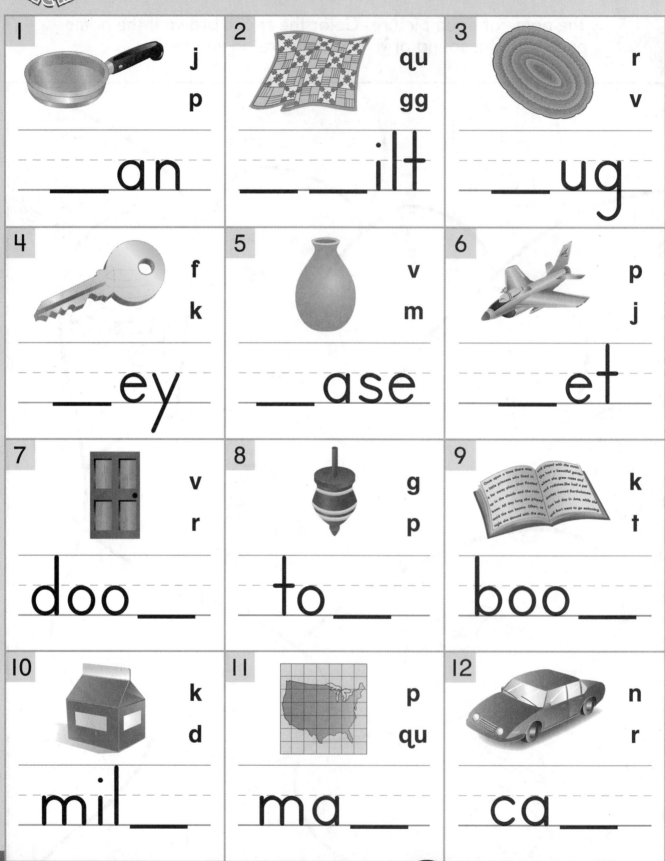

1 j p

__ an

2 qu gg

__ ilt

3 r v

__ ug

4 f k

__ ey

5 v m

__ ase

6 p j

__ et

7 v r

doo __

8 g p

to __

9 k t

boo __

10 k d

mil __

11 p qu

ma __

12 n r

ca __

LESSON 30: Reviewing Initial and Final
Consonants **p, r, k, j, q(u), v**

PHONICS Alive at Home

Help your child draw 12 squares to look like a quilt. Fill in each square with a word that begins with **p, r, k, j, q(u),** or **v.**

Year starts with the sound of **y.** **Zero** starts with the sound of **z.** Listen for the sounds of **y** and **z** in the rhyme.

Count down to zero.
Yell out a loud cheer.
The old year is out.
The new year is here.

First color each picture that has the sound of **y** at the beginning of its name ▭▷. Then color each picture that has the sound of **z** at the beginning of its name ▭.

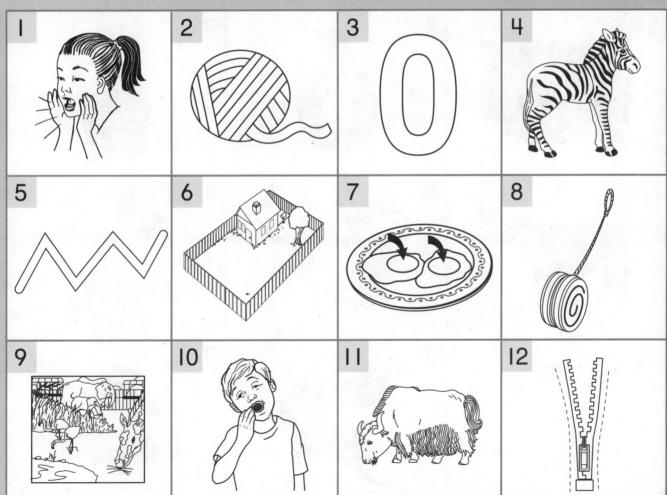

X ZZ

Box ends with the sound of **x. Fuzz** ends with the sound of **z.**
Listen for the sounds of **x** and **z** in the rhyme.

A toy with fuzz,
Bugs that buzz,
A box of clay, a sax to play,
I love a fun piñata day!

Put an **X** on each picture that has the sound of **x** at the end
of its name. Then circle each picture that has the sound
of **z** at the end of its name.

1	2	3
4	5	6
7	8	9

LESSON 31: Phonemic Awareness: Final /ks/ and /z/

With your child, find things that buzz
in your home and say **buzz**. Repeat
with things you mix and say **mix**.

Say the name of each picture. Circle the letter or letters that stand for the missing sound. Then print the letter or letters on the line.

1 k v a n	**2** z y o o	**3** f k e y
4 p j e n	**5** qu y a r n	**6** r z u g
7 g qu e e n	**8** j p e t	**9** v x f o
10 p k t o	**11** k t b o o	**12** r x c a

Say the name of each picture. Find the letter or letters in the box that stand for the missing sound. Then print the letter or letters on the line.

p	r	k	j	qu	v	x	y	z

1 ___it

2 ___ase

3 ___ope

4 ___iet

5 ___ot

6 ___ell

7 ___eep

8 ___ero

9 bo___

10 fou___

11 ma___

12 hoo___

LESSON 32: Assessing Initial and Final
Consonants p, r, k, j, q(u), v, x, y, z

Review this Check-Up with your child.

Say the name of each picture. Draw a line from each picture to the letters that stand for its ending sound.

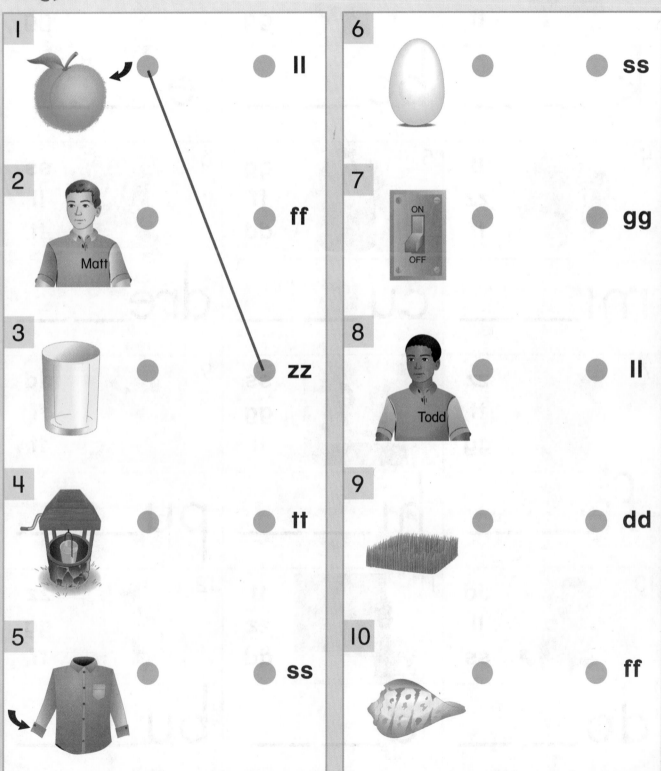

Check-Up

Say the name of each picture. Circle the letters that stand for its ending sound. Then print the letters on the lines.

1	ff ss tt	2	ll tt gg	3	zz dd gg
ki___		be___		e___	

4	ll zz tt	5	gg ff dd	6	ss ll tt
mi___		cu___		dre___	

7	zz tt gg	8	ss gg ll	9	dd ff tt
fi___		hi___		pu___	

10	dd ll ss	11	tt zz dd	12	zz gg ff
do___		a___		bu___	

LESSON 33: Assessing Double Final Consonants
ff, ss, tt, ll, dd, gg, zz

Review this Check-Up with your child.

Summer has the sound of **m** in the middle. Listen for the middle consonant sounds in the rhyme.

Bobbing for apples,
A three-legged run,
And riding on ponies,
Make summer great fun!

Circle the letter that stands for the middle consonant sound.

1	2	3	4
m (p) n	j p t	m n w	p f v

5	6	7	8
l b n	x v g	c d q	x n h

9	10	11	12
d f c	m g p	s t l	b k f

Say the name of each picture. Print the letter that stands for the middle consonant sound on the line.

1	2	3
wa_g_on	spi_er	tu_ip
4	5	6
ca_el	ca_in	wa_er
7 **7**	8 `1 2 3 4 5 6 7 8 9 10 11 12`	9
se_en	ru_er	le_on
10	11	12
sa_ad	ro_in	po_y

LESSON 34: Recognizing and Writing
Medial Consonants

PHONICS
Alive at Home

Say **l, d, g, m, b, n, v,** or **t,** and have your child point to a picture with that letter in the middle of its name.

Look and Learn

Listen as the page is read aloud.
Look at the pictures. Then talk
about what you see.

We can celebrate in
many ways. We can have
a parade. We can also
make food, sing songs,
and wear costumes.
The people in the pictures
are celebrating the new
year. They made a big
dragon.

How do you celebrate
special times?

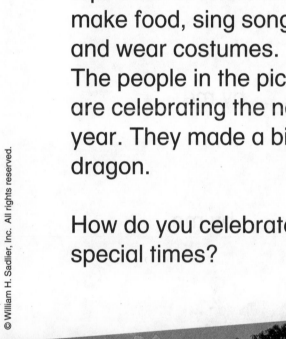

The words in the box are often used in sentences.
Use one of the words to complete each sentence.
Then practice reading the sentences aloud.

| by | funny | Let | ride | Stop | walk |

1. The 🐕🐕 run _____ me.

2. The 🐻🐻 _____ by me.

3. The 🤡🤡 _____ by me.

4. I like the _____ 🤡🤡 .

5. _____ ! Let me walk with you.

6. _____ me be funny, too!

Print each word from the box on a piece of paper. Have your child match each word to the same word in the sentences.

Say the name of each picture. Print the letter that stands for the missing sound on the line.

1	2	3
le__on	sea__	__ish
4	5	6
ru__	__og	ca__in
7	8	9
__oo	spi__er	we__
10	11	12
pea__ut	po__	__eep

Check-Up

Say the name of each picture. Print the letter that stands for the missing sound on the line.

1 fo___	2 ___un	3 wa___er
4 ___an	5 sa___ad	6 li___
7 wa___on	8 quee___	9 ___en
10 mo___	11 se___en	12 ___eam

LESSON 37: Assessing Initial, Final, and
Medial Consonants

Review this Check-Up with your child.

Read Aloud

BUGS

I like bugs.
Black bugs,
Green bugs,
Bad bugs,
Mean bugs,
Any kind of bug,

A bug in a rug,
A bug in the grass,
A bug on the sidewalk,
A bug in a glass—
I like bugs.

Round bugs,
Shiny bugs,
Fat bugs,
Buggy bugs,
Big bugs,
Ladybugs,
I like bugs.

Margaret Wise Brown

Critical Thinking

How are these bugs different?
How do different kinds of bugs move?

LESSON 38: Short Vowels
Phonemic Awareness: Segmenting Words

Name _____

Dear Family,

In this unit, your child will learn the sounds of the short vowels. She or he will also be thinking and reading about bugs. As your child progresses through this unit, you can make phonics come alive at home with these activities.

• Look at the pictures below. Say each letter and picture name with your child. Listen to the vowel sound.

Apreciada Familia:

En esta unidad los niños aprenderán los sonidos cortos de las vocales. También pensarán y leerán sobre insectos. A medida que se avanza ustedes pueden revivir los fonemas en la casa con estas actividades.

• Miren los grabados. Pronuncien juntos cada letra y el nombre del objeto. Escuchen el sonido de la vocal.

a	i	o	u	e
			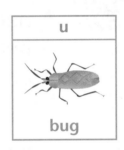	
cat	six	box	bug	bed

• Read the poem "Bugs" on the reverse side of this page as your child follows along. Talk about the bugs you see.

• Help your child find some of the short vowel words in the poem, such as **bugs**, **black**, **bad**, **rug**, **on**, **glass**, **fat**, and **big**.

• Say these words one at a time: **bug**, **fat**, and **big**. Ask your child to say the three sounds heard in each word. (b-u-g, f-a-t, b-i-g)

• Lea el poema "Bugs" en la página 77 mientras su hijo lo repite. Hablen acerca de los insectos que ven.

• Ayude al niño a encontrar algunas vocales de sonido corto en las palabras del poema, tales como: **bugs, black, bad, rug, on, glass, fat** y **big**.

• Pronuncie estas palabras una por una: **bug, fat** y **big**. Pida al niño decir el sonido en cada palabra. (b-u-g, f-a-t, b-i-g)

PROJECT

Use your imagination to draw a "never seen before" bug. Will it have spots? What kind of wings will it have? Give your new bug a name. Next to your picture, print five or six words that describe it.

PROYECTO

Dibujen un "insecto nunca visto". ¿Tendrá motitas? ¿Qué tipo de alas tendrá? Pónganle un nombre al nuevo insecto. Escriban cinco o seis palabras para describirlo.

Listen Listen as the page is read aloud. Talk about the short **a** words you hear, such as **can** and **pack.** Then act out the story.

I Can

I **can pack** a **bag.**
An ant can't.

I **can tag** a **pal.**
An ant can't.

I **can clap** my **hands.**
An ant can't.

I **can** hide in the **grass.**
And an ant can, too!

Critical Thinking

What are some things an ant can do that you can't?

Cat has the short **a** sound. Print **a** on the line under each picture that has the short **a** sound in its name.

 Short **a**

1	2
3	4
5	6
7	8
9	10
11	12
13	14
15	16

LESSON 39: Connecting Sound to Symbol: /a/ a

Say the name of each picture. Ask your child to tag you if the name has the short **a** sound.

Trace the line as you blend the sounds together to say the word. Then circle the picture it names.

1	**v a n** →				

2	**t a g** →				

3	**h a m** →				

4	**c a t** →				

5	**m a p** →				

LESSON 40: Blending with Short Vowel **a**

81

★ Trace the line as you blend the sounds together to say the word. Then print the word under the picture it names.

j a m
- - - - - ➔

b a g
- - - - - ➔

m a t
- - - - - ➔

f a n
- - - - - ➔

c a p
- - - - - ➔

g a s
- - - - - ➔

1 	2	3
4 	5 	6 

LESSON 40: Blending with Short Vowel **a**

Clap hands with your child as he or she says the three sounds heard in each word on this page: **j-a-m**.

Say the name of each picture. In each row, circle two pictures that have rhyming names. Then make a new rhyming word.

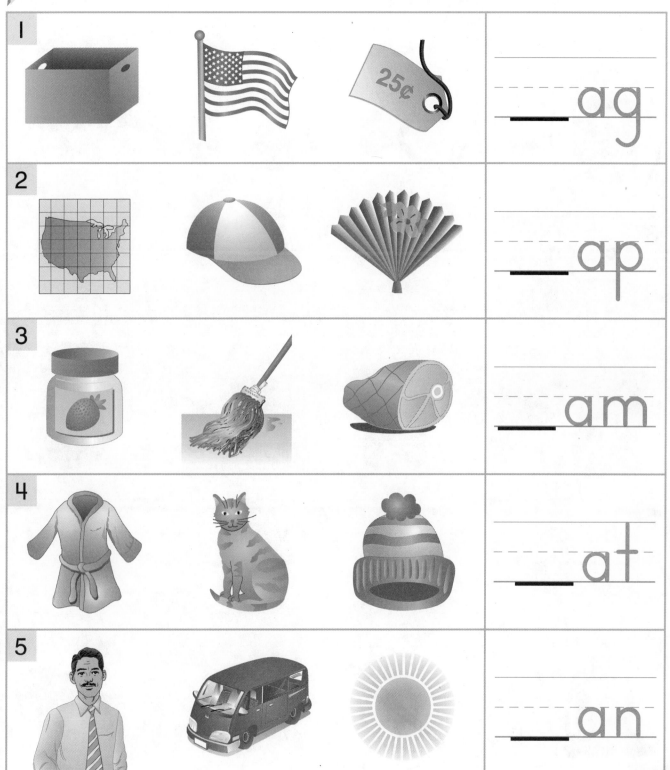

1. _____ag

2. _____ap

3. _____am

4. _____at

5. _____an

1

b ag _____ bag

2

c ap _____

3

c an _____

4

h am _____

5

b at _____

6

v an _____

LESSON 41: Blending with Short Vowel **a** Phonograms

Have your child select one word on the page and together build a list of rhyming words.

Trace the line as you blend the sounds together to say the word. Then print the word under the picture it names.

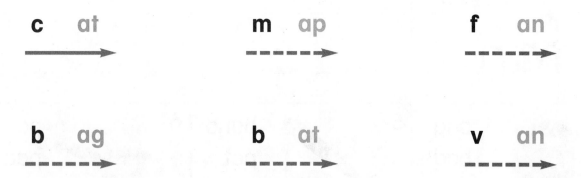

c **at**

m **ap**

f **an**

b **ag**

b **at**

v **an**

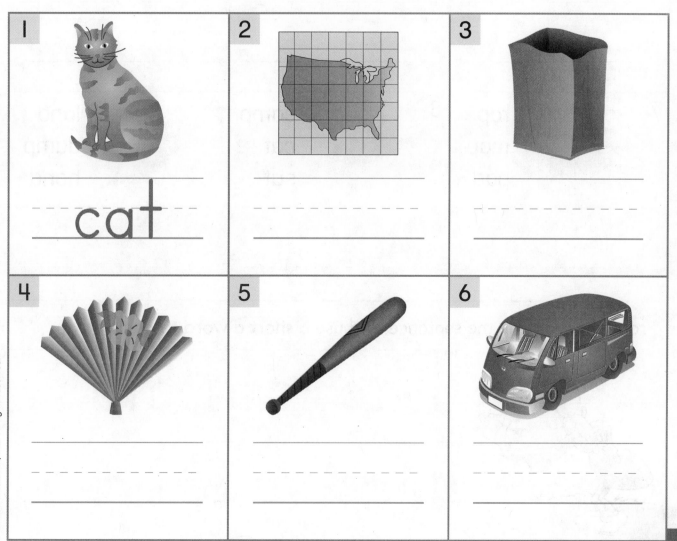

1. cat

2.

3.

4.

5.

6.

Circle the name of the picture and print it on the line.

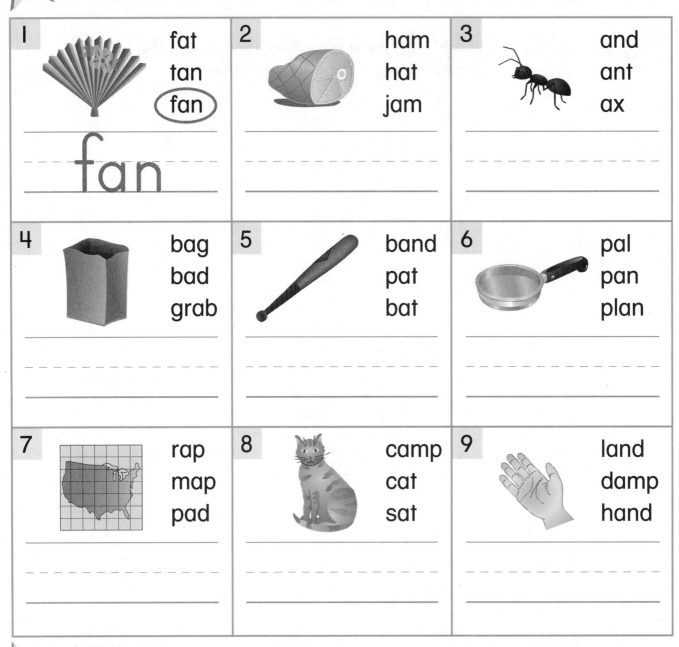

1
fat
tan
(fan)

fan

2
ham
hat
jam

3
and
ant
ax

4
bag
bad
grab

5
band
pat
bat

6
pal
pan
plan

7
rap
map
pad

8
camp
cat
sat

9
land
damp
hand

Trace the words in the sentence and use a short **a** word to complete it.

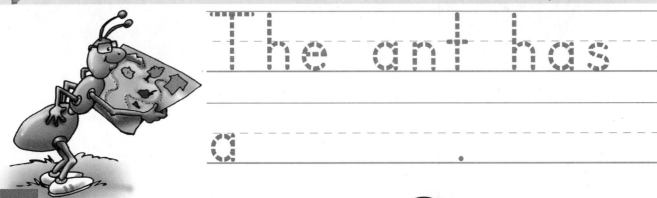

The ant has

a

LESSON 42: Writing Short Vowel **a**

Fold a sheet of paper like an accordion to make a fan. Help your child write a short **a** word on each pleat.

Pat can nap.

8

Name _____

PAT

Fold

This is Pat.

I

Pat can tap.

6

Fold

Pat can ride.

3

Directions: Cut and fold the book. Then read the story. Tell all of the different things Pat does in the story.

Pat can run.

Pat can stop.

2

Pat can jump.

Pat can bat.

LESSON 43: Short Vowel **a** Decodable Reader
Comprehension: Recalling Details

Look at each picture. Circle the word that completes the sentence. Then print it on the line.

1. Dan got his ___ **bat** ___ .

   fat
   (bat)
   bad

2. He _____ up the hill.

   rap
   pan
   ran

3. His _____ fell off.

   cap
   cat
   can

4. Dan _____ on the log.

   sat
   rat
   mat

5. He felt a bug on his _____ .

   ham
   sand
   hand

6. It was just a little _____ .

   ax
   ant
   tan

My Ant Farm

My pet ants
Snack on jam.
Their names are
Ann, Pam, and Sam.

I hand them
Scraps and grass.
Then I watch them
In the glass.

1. Jam is a _____ for the ants.

2. The ants are Ann, Pam, and _____.

3. You can watch them in the _____.

LESSON 44: Short Vowel **a** in Context
Comprehension: Recalling Details

Read the poem to your child. Talk about other things Ann, Pam, and Sam might do.

Remember

Use the pictures to complete the puzzle. Start in the box with the same number as the clue. Print one letter in each box.

ACROSS ➡

1. 3. 5.

1 h **a** **2** m

DOWN ⬇

2.

4.

3. **4**

5.

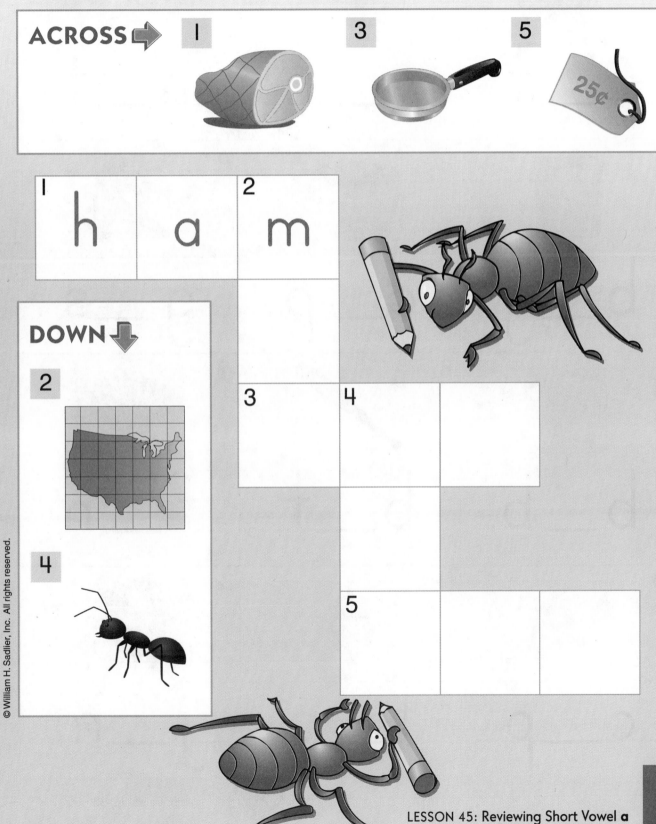

Say the name of each picture. Print **a** on the line to complete the picture name if it has the short **a** sound.

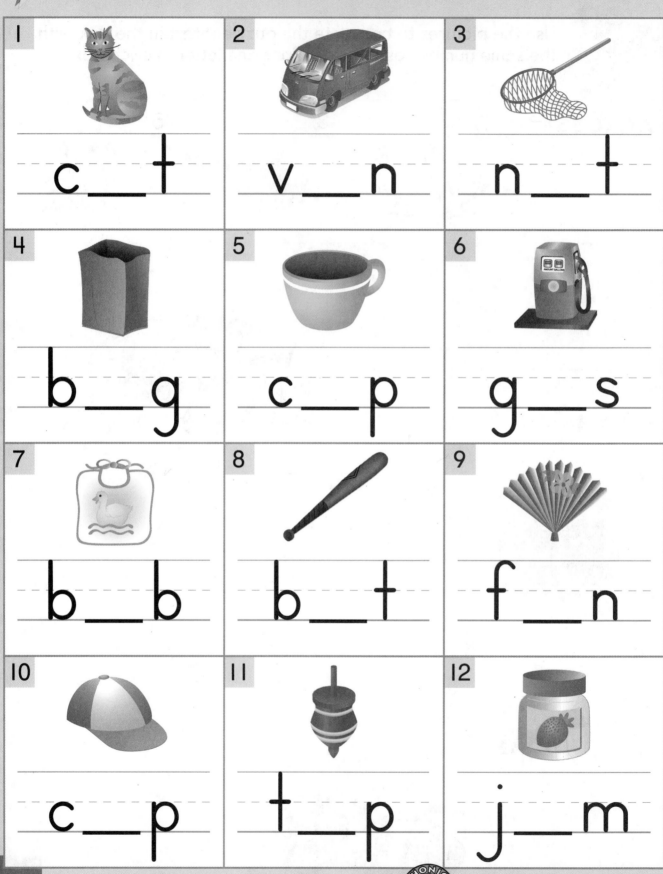

1 c_t	2 v_n	3 n_t
4 b_g	5 c_p	6 g_s
7 b_b	8 b_t	9 f_n
10 c_p	11 t_p	12 j_m

LESSON 45: Assessing Short Vowel **a**

Review this Check-Up with your child.

Listen as the page is read aloud. Talk about the short **i** words you hear, such as **it** and **sits.** Then draw the answer to the riddle at the bottom of the page.

What Is It?

It has **six** legs,
And **it** has **wings.**
Sometimes **it sits.**
Sometimes **it stings.**
What **is it?**
It is a **big**…

Critical Thinking

What are the names of some other bugs with wings?

LESSON 46: Phonemic Awareness: /i/

Six has the short **i** sound. Print **i** on the line under each picture that has the short **i** sound in its name.

1	2	3	4

5	6	7	8

9	10	11	12

13	14	15	16

LESSON 46: Connecting Sound to Symbol /i/ i

PHONICS
Alive at Home

Say the name of each picture. Ask your child to hold up six fingers if the name has the short **i** sound.

⭐ **T**race the line as you blend the sounds together to say the word. Then circle the picture it names.

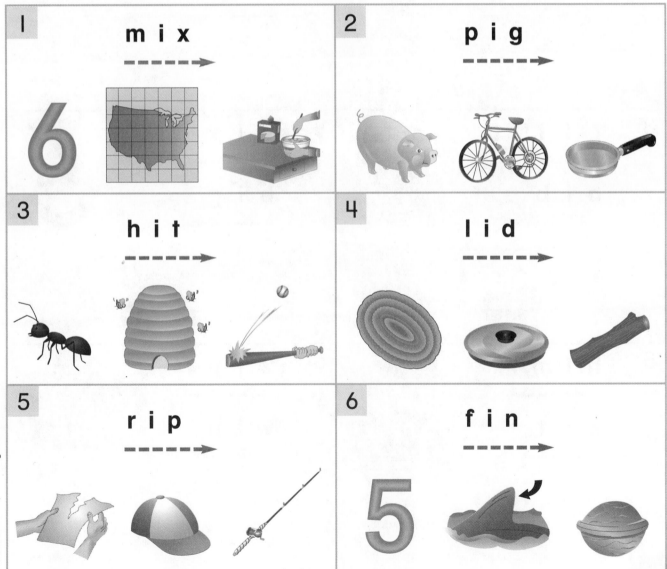

1   **m i x** →

2   **p i g** →

3   **h i t** →

4   **l i d** →

5   **r i p** →

6   **f i n** →

Trace the line as you blend the sounds together to say the word.
Then print the word that names each picture.

1	**t i p**	
	w i g	

2	**p i n**	
	d i d	

3	**f i t**	
	b i b	

4	**s i x**	
	b i g	

5	**h i m**	
	k i t	

6	**z i p**	
	w i n	

LESSON 47: Blending with Short Vowel **i**

Have your child retrace the arrow
slowly with a pencil or crayon as
you blend each word.

Say the name of each picture. In each row, circle two pictures that have rhyming names. Then make a new rhyming word.

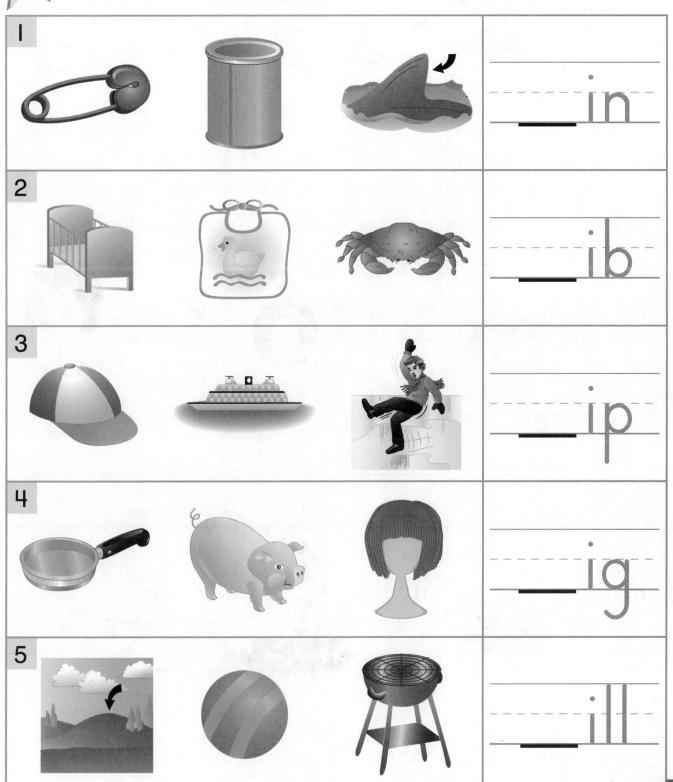

1. _____ in

2. _____ ib

3. _____ ip

4. _____ ig

5. _____ ill

1

f   in

- - - - →

2

b   ib

- - - - →

3

p   in

- - - - →

4

l   id

- - - - →

5

s   ix

- - - - →

6

6

w   ig

- - - - →

7

m   ix

- - - - →

8

d   ig

- - - - →

9

r   ip

- - - - →

PHONICS Alive at Home

Let your child teach you how to use the arrows to blend the words on the page.

I   r   ip   _____

2   s   ix   _____

3   b   ib   _____

4   v   an   _____

5   b   at   _____

6   p   in   _____

LESSON 49: Blending with Phonograms

99

ircle the word that names each picture.

1 win will tin	**2** fit sink six	**3** hill gift grill
4 pin fix fin	**5** ham hit hat	**6** pit pig wig
7 bit fib bib	**8** pit pan pin	**9** cat bit bat
10 hill will him	**11** wag wig win	**12** pin pan pat
13 bag big bug	**14** mitt mat milk	**15** laps sip lips

Read a circled word. Have your child say the word slowly, separating the initial sound from the rest of the word: **w in.**

Circle the name of the picture and print it on the line.

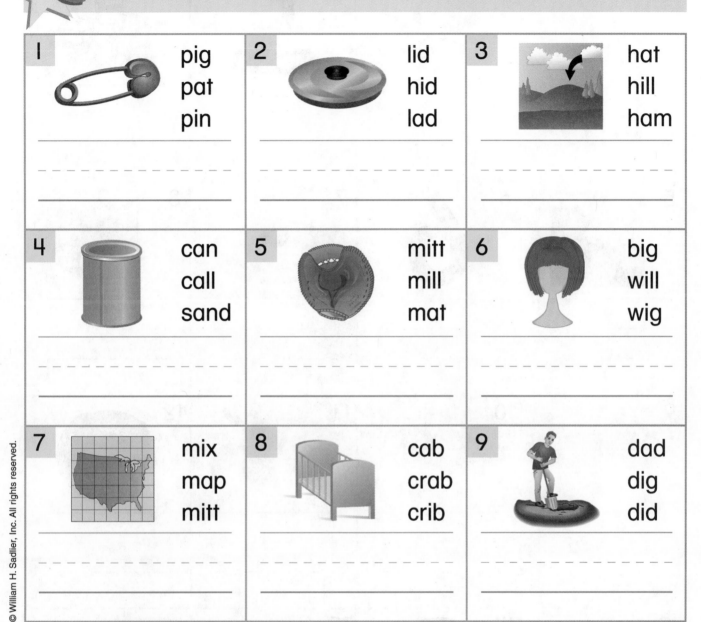

1	pig pat pin	2	lid hid lad	3	hat hill ham
4	can call sand	5	mitt mill mat	6	big will wig
7	mix map mitt	8	cab crab crib	9	dad dig did

Trace the words in the sentence and use a short **i** word to complete it.

The ant is

on a _____ .

1 bib	2	3	4
5	6	7	8
9	10	11	12
13	14	15	16

Ask your child to read the words. Work together to make up sentences for three of the words.

8 Sid did fix it!

I Can Read

Your child has read this book in school. Ask him or her to read it to you. Then have your child find, spell, and read each short **i** word in the story.

Name _____

Fix It!

Can Sid fix the mitt? I

6 Sid did fix it!

Can Sid fix the wig? 3

Directions: Cut and fold the book. Read the story. Tell about each problem and how it was solved.

 LESSON 51: Short Vowel **i** Decodable Reader
Comprehension: Identifying Problem/Solution

2   Sid did fix it!

Can Sid fix the big rip?   7

4   Sid did fix it!

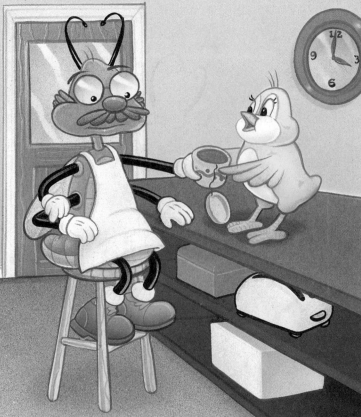

Can Sid fix the lid?   5

LESSON 51: Short Vowel **i** Decodable Reader
Comprehension: Identifying Problem/Solution

1		Lin ___**sits**___ still.	hits six (sits)
2		A bug _____ in the grass.	is kiss as
3		Lin is _____ to grab it.	bib sink quick
4		Lin has the bug _____ the jar.	is in it
5		Lin looks at _____ .	it in an
6		She lifts the _____ .	lad lid Lin

Listen as the poem is read aloud to find out about bugs. Then use short **i** words to complete the sentences.

What Is a Bug?

Some bugs have six legs,
Not more than six!
Some bugs have odd names,
Like walkingsticks.

Insects can have wings,
And some can sting!
It seems bugs can do
All kinds of things.

_____
- - - - - - - - - - - - - - -

1. Some bugs have _____ legs.

_____
- - - - - - - - - - - - - - -

2. Bugs with _____ can fly.

_____
- - - - - - - - - - - - - - -

3. Look out for bugs that can _____ .

LESSON 52: Short Vowel **i** in Context
Comprehension: Setting a Purpose for Reading

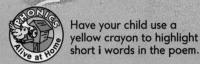

Have your child use a yellow crayon to highlight short **i** words in the poem.

Check-Up

Say the name of each picture. Print **i** on the line to complete the picture name if it has the short **i** sound.

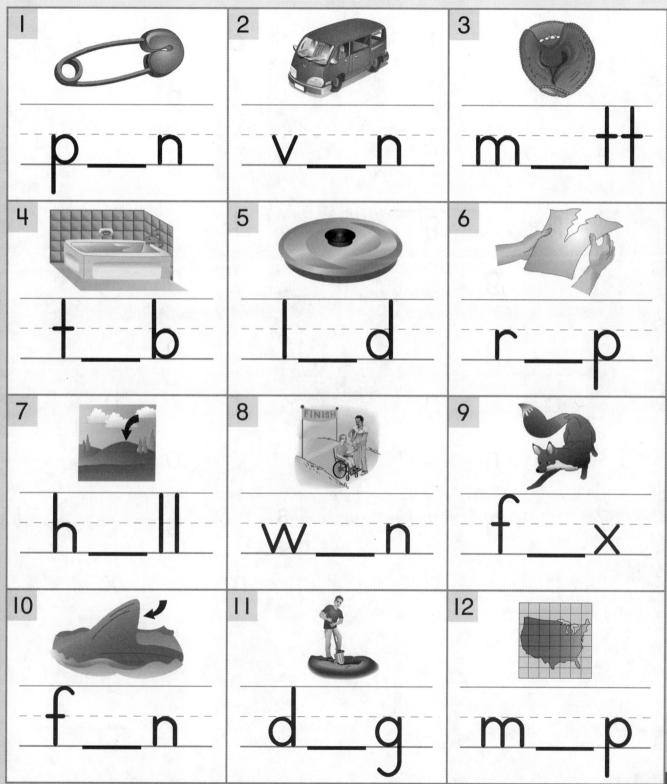

1 p_n	2 v_n	3 m_tt
4 t_b	5 l_d	6 r_p
7 h_ll	8 w_n	9 f_x
10 f_n	11 d_g	12 m_p

Print **a** or **i** in each center box to make two words. Read the words across and down. Say the rhyming word part used in both words.

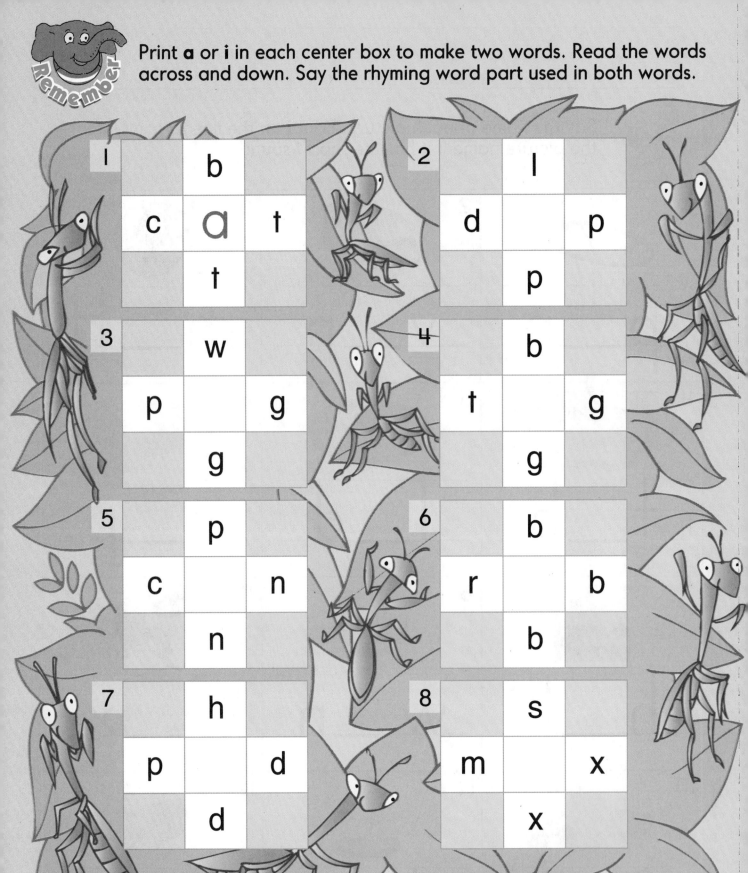

1.

	b	
c	a	t
	t	

2.

	l	
d		p
	p	

3.

	w	
p		g
	g	

4.

	b	
t		g
	g	

5.

	p	
c		n
	n	

6.

	b	
r		b
	b	

7.

	h	
p		d
	d	

8.

	s	
m		x
	x	

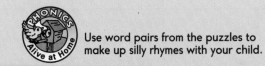

Use word pairs from the puzzles to make up silly rhymes with your child.

Listen as the page is read aloud. Talk about the short **o** words you hear, such as **hop** and **stop.** Then hop like a bug and stop like one, too.

Hop and Stop

Hop! Hop! Hop!
Time to **stop.**

Hop to the **box.**
Time to **stop.**

Jog in place.
Time to **stop.**

Isn't it fun
To **hop** and **stop!**

Critical Thinking

What are some other ways bugs can move?

Short o

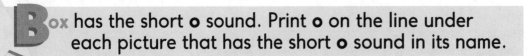

Box has the short **o** sound. Print **o** on the line under each picture that has the short **o** sound in its name.

1	2	3	4
_____	_____	_____	_____
_ _ _ _ _	_ _ _ _ _	_ _ _ _ _	_ _ _ _ _
_____	_____	_____	_____

5	6	7	8
_____	_____	_____	_____
_ _ _ _ _	_ _ _ _ _	_ _ _ _ _	_ _ _ _ _
_____	_____	_____	_____

9	10	11	12
_____	_____	_____	_____
_ _ _ _ _	_ _ _ _ _	_ _ _ _ _	_ _ _ _ _
_____	_____	_____	_____

13	14	15	16
_____	_____	_____	_____
_ _ _ _ _	_ _ _ _ _	_ _ _ _ _	_ _ _ _ _
_____	_____	_____	_____

110 LESSON 54: Connecting Sound to Symbol: /o/ o

Say the name of each picture. Then have your child point to the picture of the box when he or she hears the short **o** sound.

Trace the line as you blend the sounds together to say the word. Then circle the picture it names.

1

t o p

- - - ▶

2

f o x

- - - ▶

3

l o g

- - - ▶

4

r o d

- - - ▶

5

h o t

- - - ▶

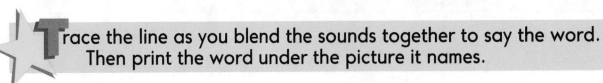

race the line as you blend the sounds together to say the word.
Then print the word under the picture it names.

c o t

r o d

d o g

h o p

f o x

m o p

l o g

p o t

c o b

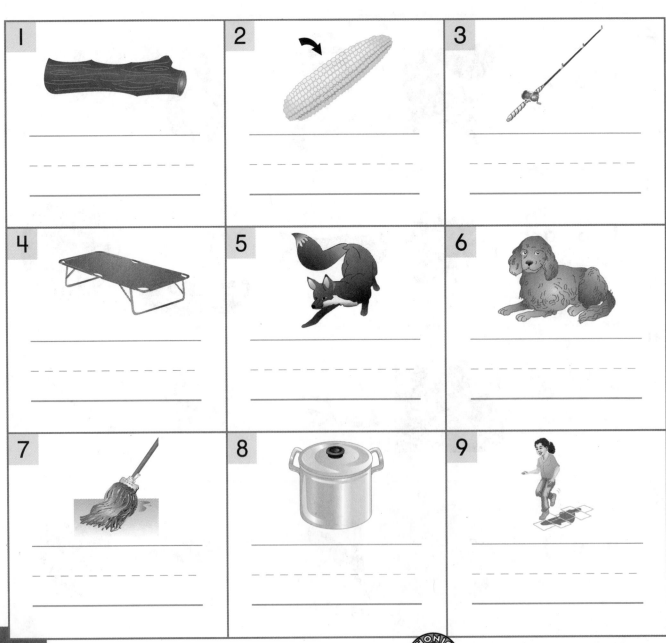

LESSON 55: Blending with Short Vowel o

Say words like **pop,** dad, **not,** mess, **mom,**
jog, jet, and **top.** Have your child hop
when he or she hears a short **o** word.

⭐ **S**ay the name of each picture. In each row, circle two pictures that have rhyming names. Then make a new rhyming word.

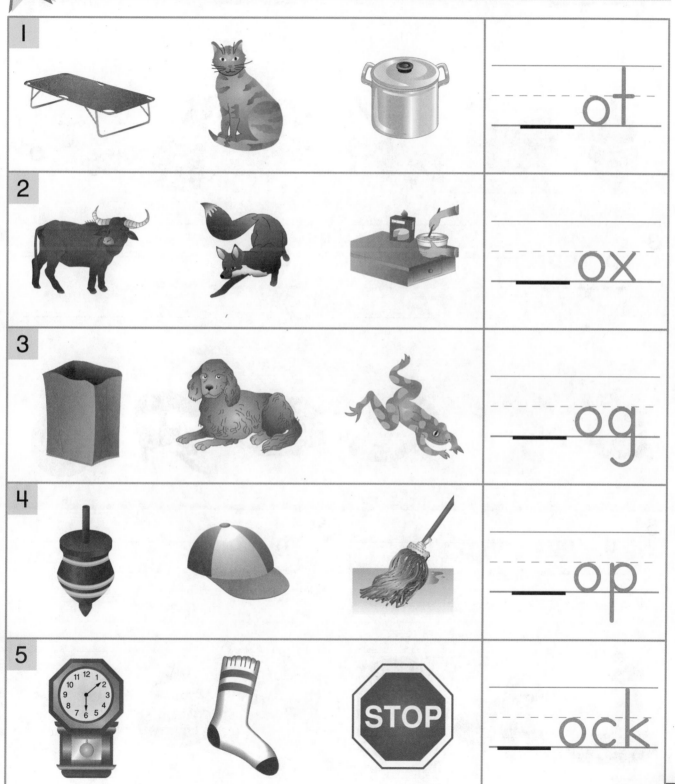

#				
1				___ot
2				___ox
3				___og
4				___op
5				___ock

1

m op _____

_____

2

c ob _____

_____

3

p op _____

_____

4

b ox _____

_____

5

d og _____

_____

6

h ot _____

_____

For review, have your child tell you the vowel sound in each picture name.

Trace the line as you blend the sounds together to say the word. Then print the word under the picture it names.

p   ot
s   ix
t   op

c   ap
l   og
h   op

f   ox
c   ot
c   at

1	**2**	**3**
4	**5**	**6**
7	**8**	**9**

_op	_ot	_ock
1	4	7
2	5	8
3	6	9

LESSON 57: Word Building with
Short Vowel o Phonograms

Read any two words. Have your child
tell whether or not the words rhyme.

1	2	3
hop mop hip	log lock block	ox fix fox

4	5	6
pot pond pan	pit pot pat	stop top tip

7	8	9
top tap pot	rock sick sock	log dog dig

10	11	12
mop pop pin	lock lick sock	map top mop

Circle the name of the picture and print it on the line.

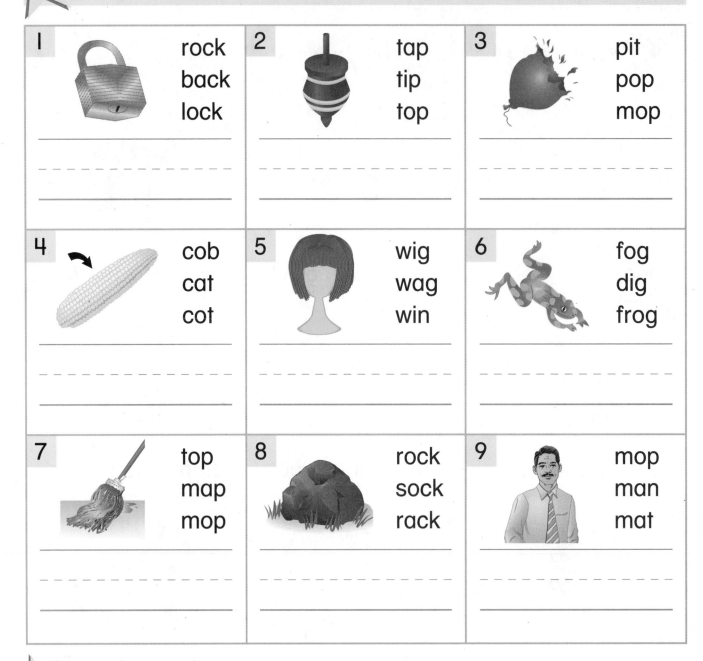

1
rock
back
lock

_____

2
tap
tip
top

_____

3
pit
pop
mop

_____

4
cob
cat
cot

_____

5
wig
wag
win

_____

6
fog
dig
frog

_____

7
top
map
mop

_____

8
rock
sock
rack

_____

9
mop
man
mat

_____

Trace the words in the sentence and use a short **o** word to complete it.

The bug hid

from the _____ .

LESSON 58: Writing Short Vowel **o**

Have your child read the sentence and name the short **o** word in it.

Name _____

Jog with Me

Fold

8 Run!

Jog with me.   1

Fold

6 Stop! Stop! Stop!

Jog by a big log.   3

Directions: Cut and fold the book. Then read the story. Tell what happens to the bugs in the book.

LESSON 59: Short Vowel **o** Decodable Reader
Comprehension: Summarizing

119

2   **Do not walk.**

Do not jog.   7

4   **Jog by a funny dog.**

Jog by a pig with a mop.   5

LESSON 59: Short Vowel **o** Decodable Reader
Comprehension: Summarizing

ook at each picture. Then print the correct sentence part on the line.

on the log.	on the rock.	on the top.
in the sock.	in the box.	

1 Where is the bug?

It is on the top.

2 Where is the bug?

It is _____

3 Where is the bug?

It is _____

4 Where is the bug?

It is _____

5 Where is the bug?

It is _____

Listen as the story is read aloud. Look at the picture. Number the sentences at the bottom to show the correct order.

Hop, Bug, Hop!

Hop, Bug, hop!
1 Hop past Pop.
2 Hop to the blocks.
3 Hop in the box.
4 Hop over the dog.
5 Hop up on the log.

Stop, Bug, stop!
Don't hop in the pond.

_____ The bug hops over the dog.

_____ The bug hops to the blocks.

_____ The bug hops past Pop.

_____ The bug hops up on the log.

_____ The bug hops in the box.

LESSON 60: Short Vowel **o** in Context
Comprehension: Sequencing

Read the story aloud. Stop before the last word in each line to let your child say the short **o** word.

Check-Up Say the name of each picture. Print **o** on the line to complete the picture name if it has the short **o** sound.

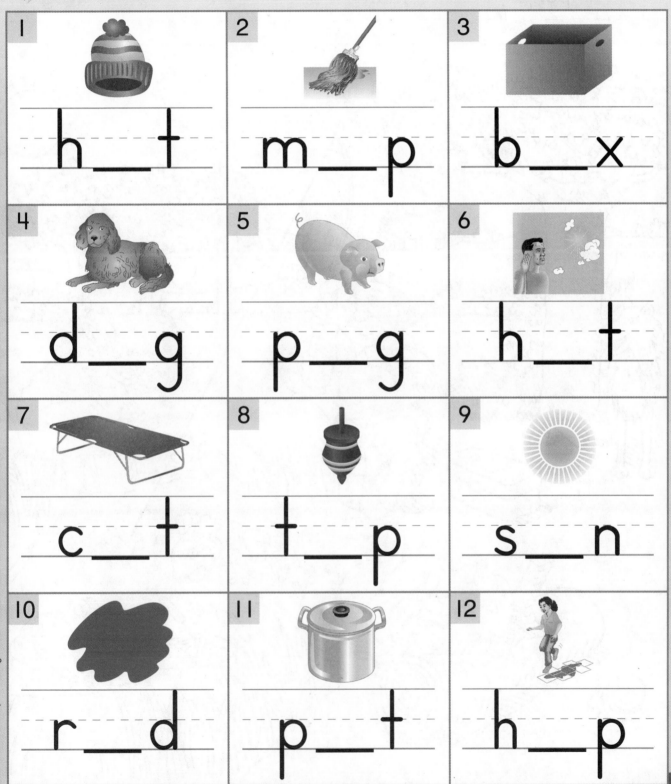

1 h_t	2 m_p	3 b_x
4 d_g	5 p_g	6 h_t
7 c_t	8 t_p	9 s_n
10 r_d	11 p_t	12 h_p

LESSON 61: Assessing Short Vowel **o**   123

Read the words in the box. Color the picture each word names.

fox	log	rock	hat
pond	man	fin	frog

LESSON 61: Reviewing Short Vowels **a, i, o**

Help your child point out pictures
of short **o** words on the page and
tell a story about the scene.

Check-Up Say the name of each picture. Circle the word and print it on the line.

1	lad lid log	2	mitt mop map	3	cob cab cat
4	pop rip pat	5	doll hill hat	6	box bit bat
7	fin fan fox	8	six box bag	9	wag man win
10	dig dad dog	11	hat hit hot	12	can fin cot

 **Check-Up** Say the name of each picture. Circle the word and print it on the line.

1 WELCOME	mat mop mitt
2	tip tap top
3	dog wig wag
4	cot cat can
5	pot pin pan
6	six fox sat
7	cob bat bib
8	lap pig log
9 25¢	top tag wig
10	fix fox fan
11	pig bag pot
12	cap lip cob

LESSON 62: Assessing Short Vowels **a, i, o**

Review this Check-Up with your child.

Listen as the page is read aloud. Talk about the short **u** words you hear, such as **bug** and **rug**. Then color the bugs.

A Snug Bug

One little **bug**
In the middle of a **rug**.
Poor little **bug**
Isn't very **snug**.

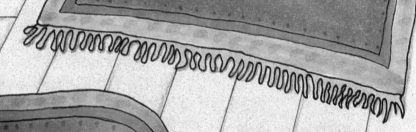

Tug, bug, tug!
Roll up the **rug**.
Soon you'll be
Cozy and **snug**.

Critical Thinking

Where else would a bug feel cozy and snug?

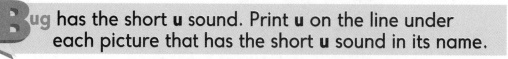 **B**ug has the short **u** sound. Print **u** on the line under each picture that has the short **u** sound in its name.

 **Short u**

1	2	3 6	4
5	6	7	8 5
9	10	11	12
13	14	15	16

128 LESSON 63: Connecting Sound to Symbol /u/ u

Name the pictures on the page. Let your child drum on a table when he or she hears a word with the short **u** sound.

⭐ **T**race the line as you blend the sounds together to say the word. Then circle the picture it names.

1 **t u b** ----→ 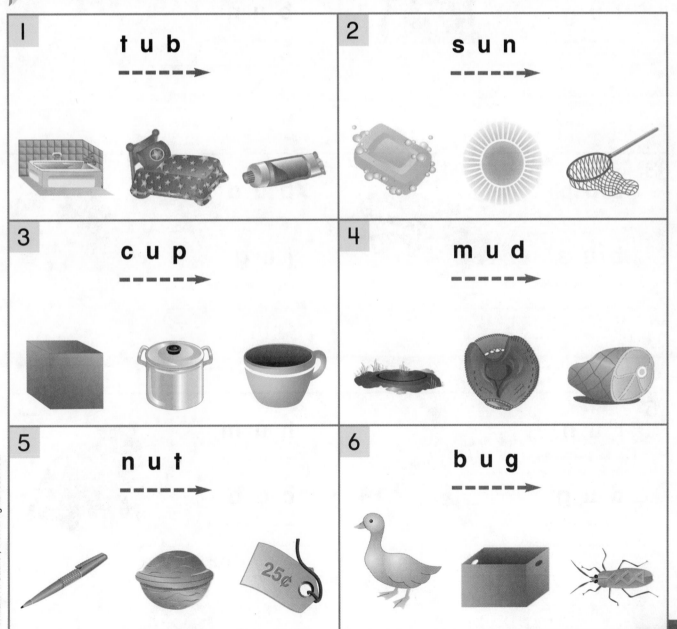	**2** **s u n** ----→
3 **c u p** ----→	**4** **m u d** ----→
5 **n u t** ----→	**6** **b u g** ----→

Trace the line as you blend the sounds together to say the word. Then print the word that names each picture.

1

h u t
------->

t u g
------->

_____
- - - - - - - - -
_____

2

g u m
------->

b u n
------->

_____
- - - - - - - - -
_____

3

c u p
------->

b u s
------->

_____
- - - - - - - - -
_____

4

b u d
------->

j u g
------->

_____
- - - - - - - - -
_____

5

r u n
------->

d u g
------->

_____
- - - - - - - - -
_____

6

h u m
------->

c u b
------->

_____
- - - - - - - - -
_____

Say the three sounds in each word, for example, **c-u-p.** Have your child put a button into a cup for each sound.

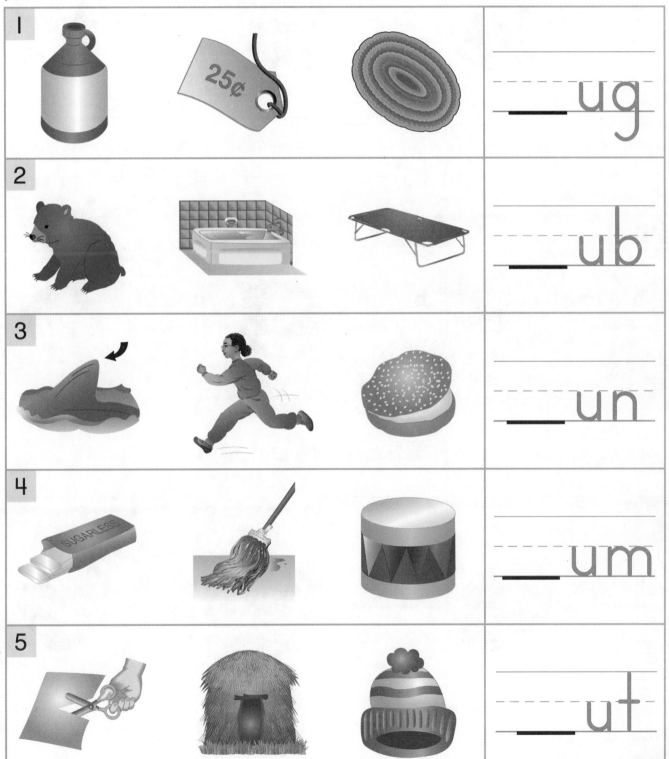

1. ___ug

2. ___ub

3. ___un

4. ___um

5. ___ut

1

c ub

2

h ut

3

p up

4

b us

5

b un

6

n ut

7

r ug

8

c up

9

h ug

LESSON 65: Blending with Short Vowel **u** Phonograms

Trace the arrow slowly with your finger as your child blends each word.

Trace the line as you blend the sounds together to say the word.
Print the word on the line. Then circle the picture it names.

1
b ud ------►

2
p ot ------►

3
m an ------►

4
j ug ------►

5
s un ------►

6
l id ------►

Say each word part. Say the name of each picture. Print the word on the line. Then add your own rhyming word and picture.

_ug	_un	_ut
1	4	7
2	5	8
3	6	9

LESSON 66: Word Building with
Short Vowel **u** Phonograms

Cut out the boxes and turn them over. With your child, take turns choosing two pictures. If the two picture names rhyme, read them aloud.

Circle the word that names each picture.

1 pop pup cup	**2** dad did dud	**3** jig jog jug
4 bug bag big	**5** mat mutt mitt	**6** cob cub cab
7 pot pat putt	**8** mud bad bud	**9** nut not rut
10 rig rag rug	**11** cap cup cut	**12** hug hog hut
13 cub tub tab	**14** cut cat cot	**15** bit but bat

Circle the name of the picture and print it on the line.

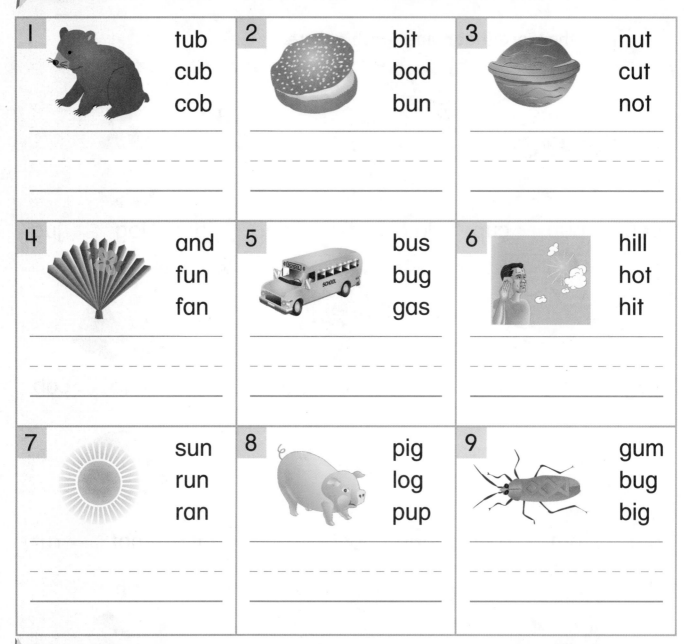

1	tub / cub / cob	2	bit / bad / bun	3	nut / cut / not
4	and / fun / fan	5	bus / bug / gas	6	hill / hot / hit
7	sun / run / ran	8	pig / log / pup	9	gum / bug / big

Trace the words in the sentence and use a short **u** word to complete it.

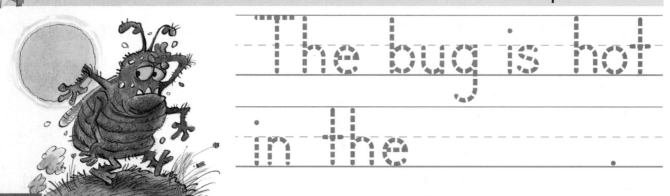

The bug is hot

in the _____.

LESSON 67: Writing Short Vowel **u**

Point to each picture on the page.
Have your child use each picture name
in a sentence.

Gus is up, but Mom is not!

8

Your child has read this book in school. Ask him or her to read it to you. Then have him or her find, spell, and read the short **u** words in the story.

Name _____

Gus and Mom

Mom is up, but Gus is not!

I

Mom will hum for Gus.

6

Mom will not let the pup jump on Gus.

3

Directions: Cut and fold the book. Then read the story. Tell where the story happens.

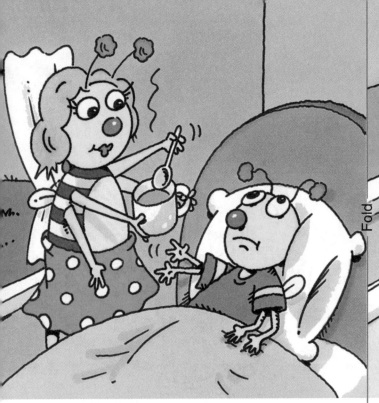

Mom will fix a cup for Gus.

2

Mom will hug Gus, too.

7

Mom will fill the tub for Gus.

4

Mom will cut the bus for Gus.

5

138

LESSON 68: Short Vowel **u** Decodable Reader
Comprehension: Identifying the Setting

ook at each picture. Circle the word that completes the sentence. Then print it on the line.

1		The _____ naps in the sun.	pup pep pop
2		"Buzz," _____ the bug.	has hams hums
3		The pup looks _____ at it.	us up as
4		It bats at the _____ .	bag beg bug
5		This is not _____ .	fit fun fat
6		The pup _____ off.	runs suns buns

LESSON 69: Short Vowel **u** in Sentences

139

A Buggy Lunch

A bug is in the cup.
A bug is on the bun.
A bug is by the pup.
Run, bugs, run.

Run, bugs, run.
Do not munch
on our lunch.

1. A bug is in the _____.

2. A bug is on the _____.

3. A bug is by the _____.

4. Do not _____ on our lunch.

LESSON 69: Short Vowel **u** in Context
Comprehension: Recalling Details

Read the poem with your child. Then ask him or her to circle all of the short **u** words.

Say the name of each picture. Print **u** on the line to complete the picture name if it has the short **u** sound.

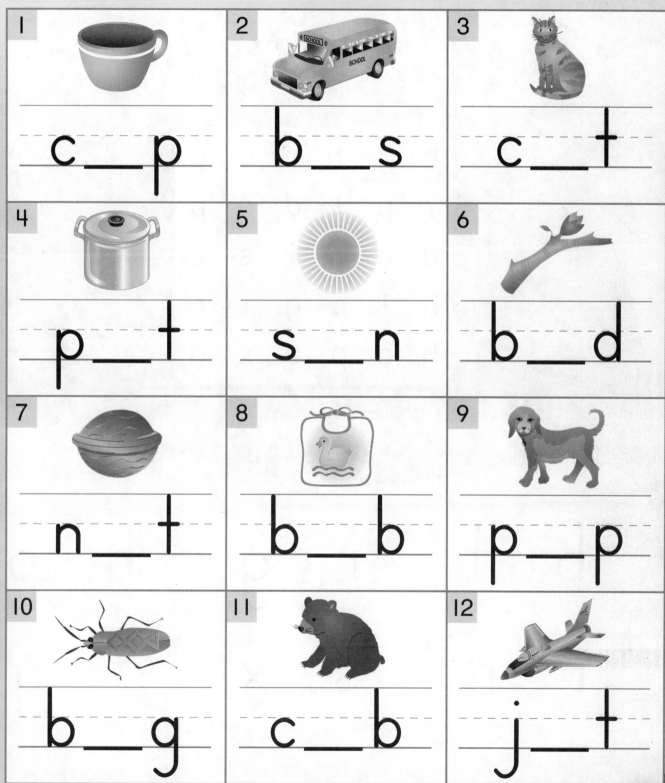

1	2	3
c _ p	b _ s	c _ t

4	5	6
p _ t	s _ n	b _ d

7	8	9
n _ t	b _ b	p _ p

10	11	12
b _ g	c _ b	j _ t

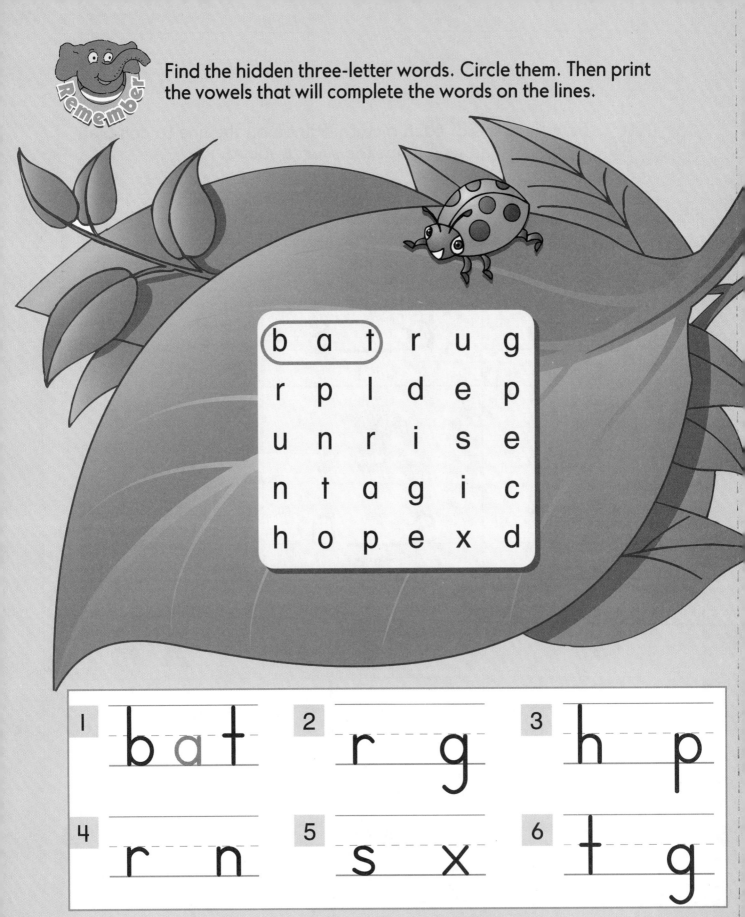

Find the hidden three-letter words. Circle them. Then print the vowels that will complete the words on the lines.

b	a	t	r	u	g
r	p	l	d	e	p
u	n	r	i	s	e
n	t	a	g	i	c
h	o	p	e	x	d

1. b a t
2. r __ g
3. h __ p
4. r __ n
5. s __ x
6. t __ g

LESSON 70: Reviewing Short Vowels **a, i, o, u**

Read aloud the words your child circled. Ask him or her to name the short vowel in each word.

Listen as the page is read aloud. Talk about the short **e** words you hear, such as **Ted** and **mess**. Then name the things under the bed. Color them Ted's favorite color—red.

Ted's Room

It's **Ted** the bug.

His room's a **mess**.

He has **ten** things

Not more, not **less**.

He hid his things

Under his **bed**.

And all the things

Ted hid are **red**.

Critical Thinking

What should Ted do to make his room look better?

Bed has the short **e** sound. Print **e** on the line under each picture that has the short **e** sound in its name.

Short **e**

1	2 **10**	3	4
5	6	7	8
9	10	11	12
13	14	15	16

144

LESSON 71: Connecting Sound to Symbol: /e/ e

Randomly name the pictures on the page. Have your child bend down if the picture name has the short **e** sound.

Trace the line as you blend the sounds together to say the word. Then circle the picture it names.

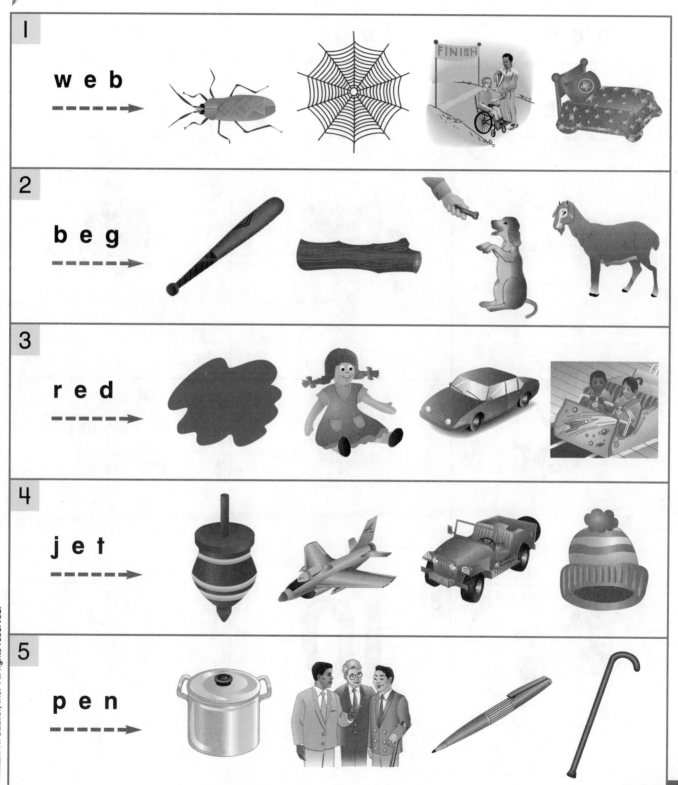

1. w e b →

2. b e g →

3. r e d →

4. j e t →

5. p e n →

Trace the line as you blend the sounds together to say each word. Then print the word under the picture it names.

p e t
- - - - - ▶

m e n
- - - - - ▶

b e d
- - - - - ▶

h e n
- - - - - ▶

l e g
- - - - - ▶

n e t
- - - - - ▶

w e b
- - - - - ▶

v e t
- - - - - ▶

t e n
- - - - - ▶

1

2

3

4

5

6

7

8   10

9

LESSON 72: Blending with Short Vowel **e**

As your child blends each word, retrace the arrow slowly with a red pen or crayon.

Say the name of each picture. In each row, circle two pictures that have rhyming names. Then make a new rhyming word.

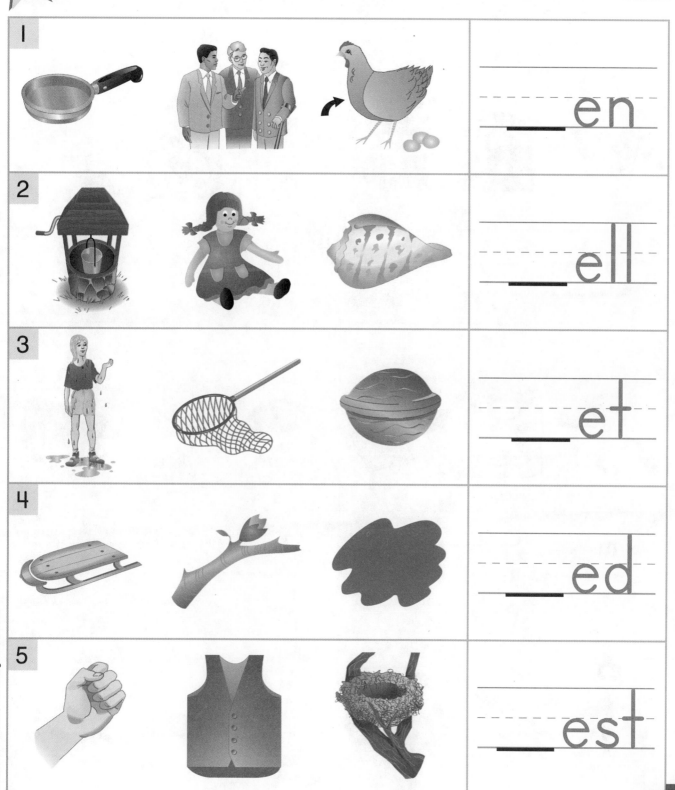

1			___en
2			___ell
3			___et
4			___ed
5			___est

Trace the line as you blend the sounds together to say the word. Print the word on the line. Then circle the picture it names.

1   h   en   _____

2   p   et   _____

3   b   ed   _____

4   n   et   _____

5   m   en   _____

6   l   eg   _____

LESSON 73: Blending with Short Vowel **e** Phonograms

Say the first sound of each word on this page. Have your child say the rest of the word. Then say the whole word together.

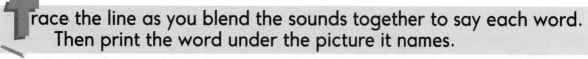

Trace the line as you blend the sounds together to say each word. Then print the word under the picture it names.

v et
- - - - →

w ell
- - - - →

r ed
- - - - →

w eb
- - - - →

n est
- - - - →

b eg
- - - - →

t en
- - - - →

b ell
- - - - →

j et
- - - - →

1 	2 	3
4 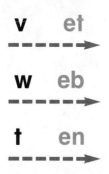	5 	6 
7 	8 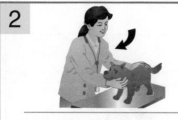	9 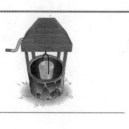

Say each word part. Say the name of each picture. Print the word on the line. Then add your own rhyming word and picture.

_en	_et	_ell
1	4	7
_____ ---------------- _____	_____ ---------------- _____	_____ ---------------- _____
2	5	8
_____ ---------------- _____	_____ ---------------- _____	_____ ---------------- _____
3	6	9
_____ ---------------- _____	_____ ---------------- _____	_____ ---------------- _____

LESSON 74: Word Building with
Short Vowel **e** Phonograms

With your child, use two words from
any column in a short rhyme like this:
Let's hop on a jet and visit a vet.

Circle the word that names each picture.

1 net not nut	**2** ten tin tan	**3** pit pet pot
4 belt bat bell	**5** nuts rest nest	**6** pen pin pan
7 rid rod red	**8** ten tent tint	**9** beg big bag
10 will well went	**11** hem ham hum	**12** jam jot jet
13 pup pep pop	**14** vest van vet	**15** bad bid bed

Circle the name of the picture and print it on the line.

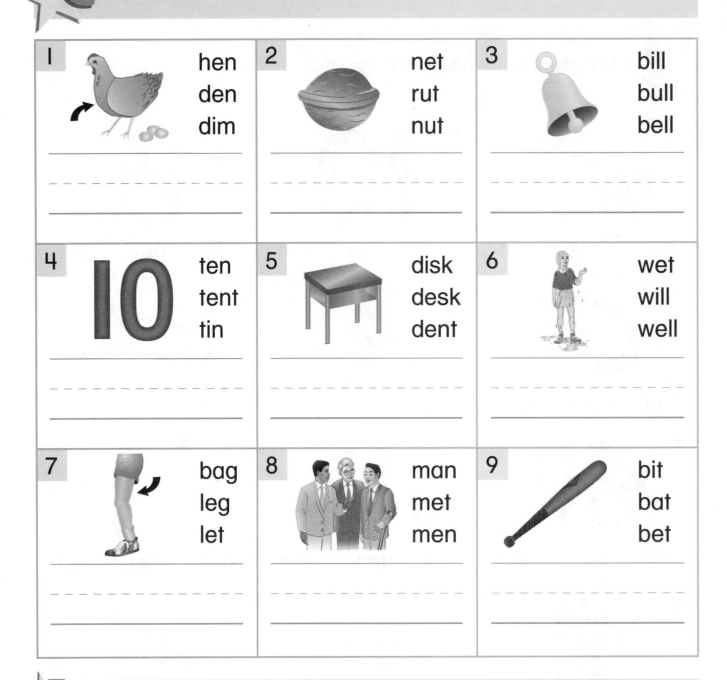

1	hen den dim	2	net rut nut	3	bill bull bell
4	ten tent tin	5	disk desk dent	6	wet will well
7	bag leg let	8	man met men	9	bit bat bet

Trace the words in the sentence and use a short **e** word to complete it.

The red bug is ____ .

LESSON 75: Writing Short Vowel **e**

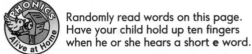

PHONICS Alive at Home

Randomly read words on this page. Have your child hold up ten fingers when he or she hears a short **e** word.

Your child has read this book in school. Ask him or her to read it to you. Then have your child make a list of all the short **e** words used in the story.

Name _____

Tell Me

Can this bug jump like you?
8 Tell me.

Is this bug wet?

I

Can this bug be a pet?

6

Is this bug red?

3

Directions: Cut and fold the book. Then read the story. Talk about other things that are wet, red, or found in a net.

LESSON 76: Short Vowel **e** Decodable Reader
Comprehension: Classifying Objects

153

Is this bug in a net?

Can this bug buzz by you?

2

7

Will this bug get fed?

Did this bug dig yet?

4

5

Look at each picture. Circle the word that completes the sentence. Then print it on the line.

1

_____

Can a bug be a _____ ?

pat
pet
pot

2

_____

_____, it can.

Yes
Yet
Jet

3

_____

It can be the _____ pet.

list
best
rest

4

_____

It will not be a _____ .

last
past
pest

5

_____

It will not make a _____ .

mess
miss
moss

6

_____

But it must be _____ .

fan
fin
fed

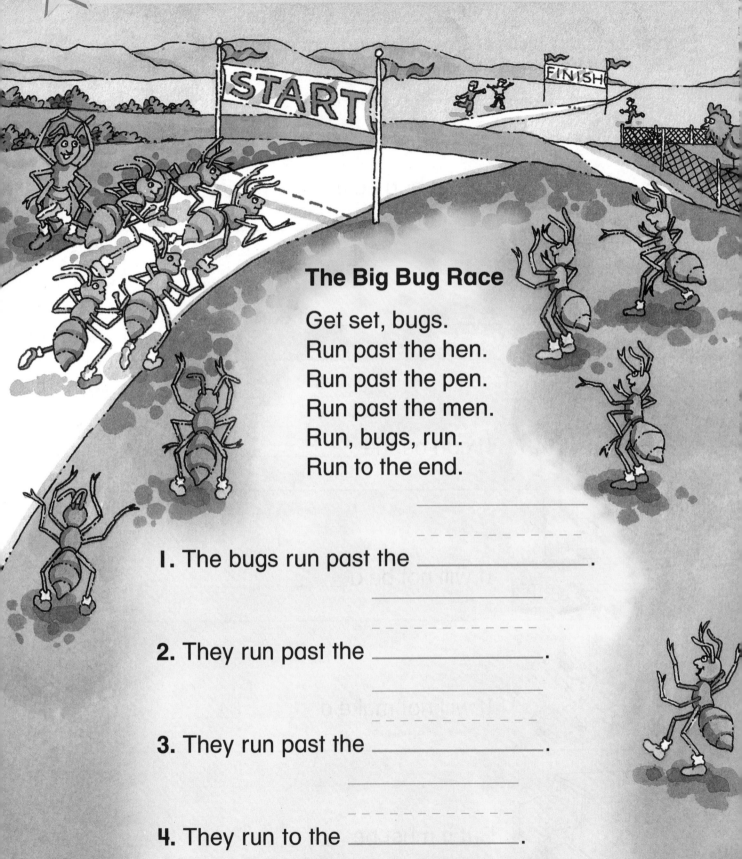

The Big Bug Race

Get set, bugs.
Run past the hen.
Run past the pen.
Run past the men.
Run, bugs, run.
Run to the end.

_____

1. The bugs run past the _____.

2. They run past the _____.

3. They run past the _____.

4. They run to the _____.

LESSON 77: Short Vowel **e** in Context
Comprehension: Retelling a Story

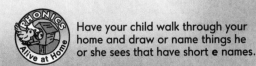

Have your child walk through your home and draw or name things he or she sees that have short **e** names.

Say the name of each picture. Print **e** on the line to complete the picture name if it has the short **e** sound.

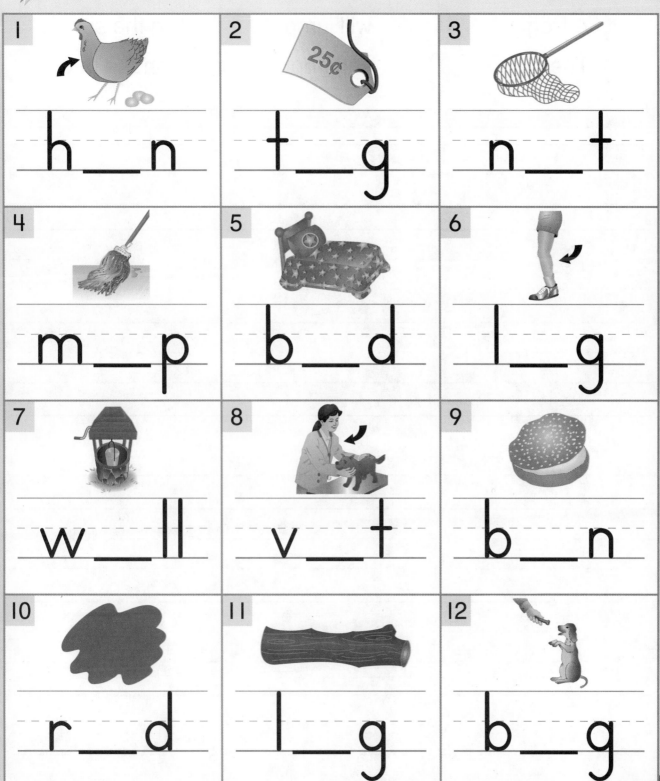

1. h_n

2. t_g

3. n_t

4. m_p

5. b_d

6. l_g

7. w_ll

8. v_t

9. b_n

10. r_d

11. l_g

12. b_g

LESSON 78: Assessing Short Vowel **e**   157

Read the words in the boxes. Combine words from boxes 1, 2, and 3 to make sentences. Print them on the lines. How many sentences can you make?

1	2	3
Six bugs	had fun	at the pond.
A frog	will jump	in the sun.
The pet	can hop	on the bud.

LESSON 78: Reviewing Short Vowels **a, i, o, u, e**

Make up silly sentences using words in the boxes. Then have your child identify the short vowel words in each.

Spell, Write, and Tell

Say, spell, and talk about each word in the box. Then print each word under the vowel sound in its name.

bug
six
bed
hat
log
fun
sit
get
had
not

Short a

1. hat
2.

Short u

7.
8.

Short i

3.
4.

Short e

9.
10.

Short o

5.
6.

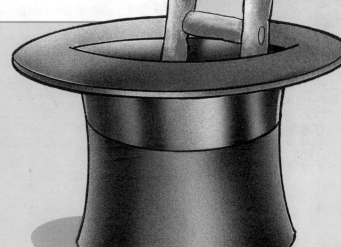

Spell, Write, and Tell

Write a sentence about each picture. Use one or more of your new spelling words in each sentence. Then tell about what you wrote.

bug		bed		log		sit		had	
	six		hat		fun		get		not

1

2

LESSON 79: Connecting Spelling, Writing, and Speaking

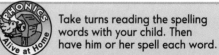

Take turns reading the spelling words with your child. Then have him or her spell each word.

Listen as the page is read aloud. Look at the pictures. Then talk about what you see.

Can you spot the bugs?
Don't let them trick you.
They can see you just fine.
Lots of bugs blend in well with
rocks, plants, and sticks.
The bugs can sit still for a very
long time. This helps them hide
and stay safe.

What can bugs do?

Treehopper

Walkingstick

Katydid

LESSON 80: Short Vowels in Context
Comprehension: Recognizing Facts

The words in the box are often used in sentences.
Use one of the words to complete each sentence.
Then practice reading the sentences aloud.

and	help	it	No	see	will

1. Do you _____ a bug by the  ?

2. Is _____ on the ?

3. _____, that bug is by the .

4. You can _____ me stop that bug.

5. I _____ run with you.

6. You _____ I will get that bug!

Print each word from the box on an index card. Have your child practice reading the words every day for a week.

Check-Up Fill in the circle next to the name of each picture.

1		2		3	
	○ pan ○ pin ○ pot		○ bed ○ bud ○ bad		○ hot ○ hut ○ hat

4		5		6	
	○ map ○ mop ○ men		○ pot ○ pat ○ pet		○ but ○ bit ○ bat

7		8		9	
	○ cut ○ cot ○ cat		○ bug ○ bill ○ bell		○ pup ○ pop ○ pep

10		11		12	
	○ dig ○ dad ○ dog		○ fin ○ fan ○ fun		○ bag ○ bug ○ beg

© William H. Sadlier, Inc. All rights reserved.

LESSON 82: Assessing Short Vowels **a, i, o, u, e**

163

 **Check-Up** Fill in the circle next to the name of each picture.

1
○ bag
○ dig
○ dog

2
○ hat
○ hot
○ hit

3
○ rug
○ rap
○ rip

4
○ beg
○ bug
○ bit

5
○ pen
○ pin
○ pan

6
○ not
○ net
○ nut

7
○ lips
○ laps
○ tops

8
○ cap
○ cob
○ cup

9
○ pat
○ pot
○ pet

10
○ fog
○ bag
○ big

11
○ bid
○ bad
○ bed

12
○ mop
○ map
○ mud

13
○ sit
○ wet
○ wag

14
○ fin
○ vet
○ van

15
○ pig
○ peg
○ pan

LESSON 82: Assessing Short Vowels **a, i, o, u, e**

Review this Check-Up with your child.

Yesterday's Paper

Yesterday's paper makes a hat,
     Or a boat,
     Or a plane,
     Or a playhouse mat.

Yesterday's paper makes things
Like that—
And a very fine tent
For a sleeping cat.

Mabel Watts

Critical Thinking

What else could you make out of old newspapers?
How might you recycle other things?

Dear Family,

As your child learns about our environment in this unit, he or she will also be learning the sounds of the long vowels. You can participate by trying these activities together at home.

● Look at the pictures below. Say each letter and picture name with your child. Listen for the long vowel sounds. (Long vowels say their own name.)

Apreciada Familia:

Mientras aprenden sobre el medio ambiente los niños también aprenderán el sonido largo de las vocales. Pueden participar de estas actividades en el hogar.

● Miren los siguientes cuadros. Pronuncien cada letra y el nombre del objeto. Escuchen el sonido largo de las vocales. (El sonido es el de su nombre.)

a	i	o	u	e
	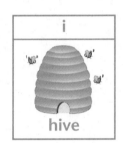			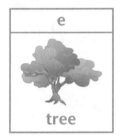
lake	hive	boat	mule	tree

● Read the poem "Yesterday's Paper" on the reverse side of this page and talk about ways to recycle.

● Help your child find long vowel words in the poem, such as **paper**, **makes**, **boat**, **plane**, **playhouse**, **like**, **fine**, and **sleeping**. Also find words that rhyme. (hat/mat/that/cat)

● Lean el poema "Yesterday's Paper" en la página 165 y hablen sobre formas de recircular.

● Ayuden al niño a encontrar vocales de sonido fuerte en el poema, tales como: **paper**, **makes**, **boat**, **plane**, **playhouse**, **like**, **fine** y **sleeping**. También busquen palabras que rimen. (hat/mat/that/cat)

PROJECT

Recycle an old shoe box and some used magazines or catalogs. Help your child cut out magazine pictures of things that have long vowel sounds in their names. Put the pictures in the box. Ask your child to sort the pictures according to the different long vowel sounds.

PROYECTO

Recirculen una caja de zapatos. Pida al niño recortar de revistas fotos de cosas que tengan vocales de sonido largo en sus nombres. Pongan las fotos en la caja. El niño puede ordenarlas de acuerdo a los diferentes sonidos.

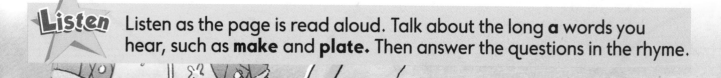

Listen Listen as the page is read aloud. Talk about the long **a** words you hear, such as **make** and **plate.** Then answer the questions in the rhyme.

What Can You Make?

What can you **make**
From a torn **paper plate,**
Or a **faded** lamp **shade,**
Or a big wooden **crate?**

What can you **save**
To use in new **ways**
To **make** things to **play** with
On cold **rainy days?**

Critical Thinking

What are some good things to save for rainy days?

LESSON 84: Phonemic Awareness: /ā/   **167**

Lake has the long **a** sound. Color the space 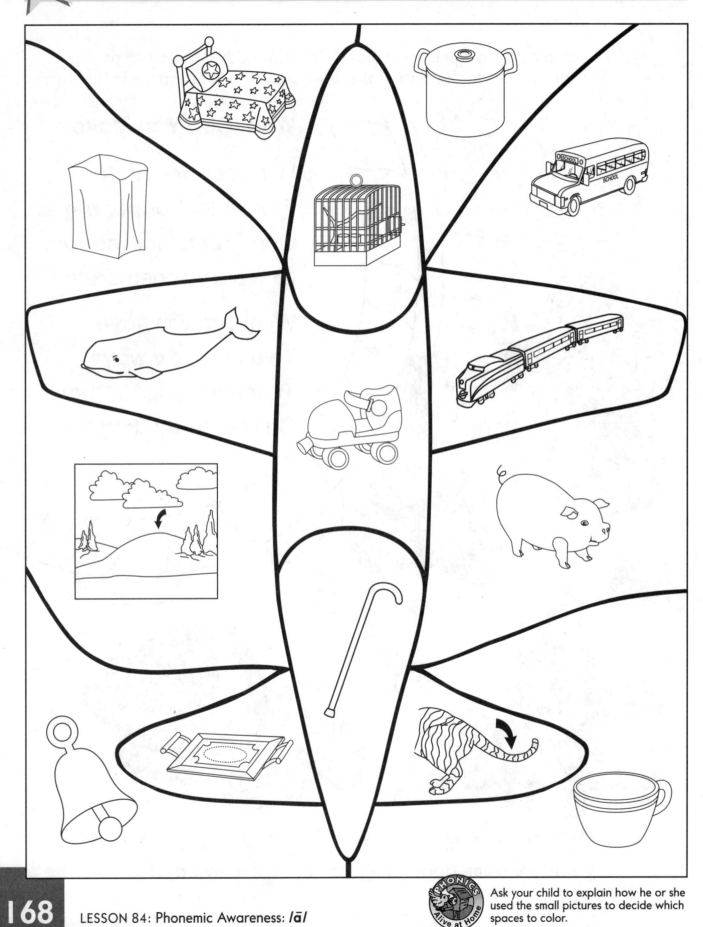 if the name of the picture has the long **a** sound. What do you see?

LESSON 84: Phonemic Awareness: /ā/

Ask your child to explain how he or she used the small pictures to decide which spaces to color.

The letters **a_e** can stand for the long **a** sound. The letter **e** is silent. Say the name of each picture. Then print **a** in the middle and **e** at the end of each word that has the long **a** sound.

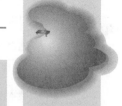

l_a_k_e

1 rake	2 g__t	3 b__t
4 d__g	5 t__p	6 c__g
7 h__n	8 v__s	9 g__m
10 w__v	11 c__p	12 wh__l

The letters **ai** and **ay** can stand for the long **a** sound. Say the name of each picture. Circle the word. Then print **ai** or **ay** on the line.

r<u>ai</u>n

h<u>ay</u>

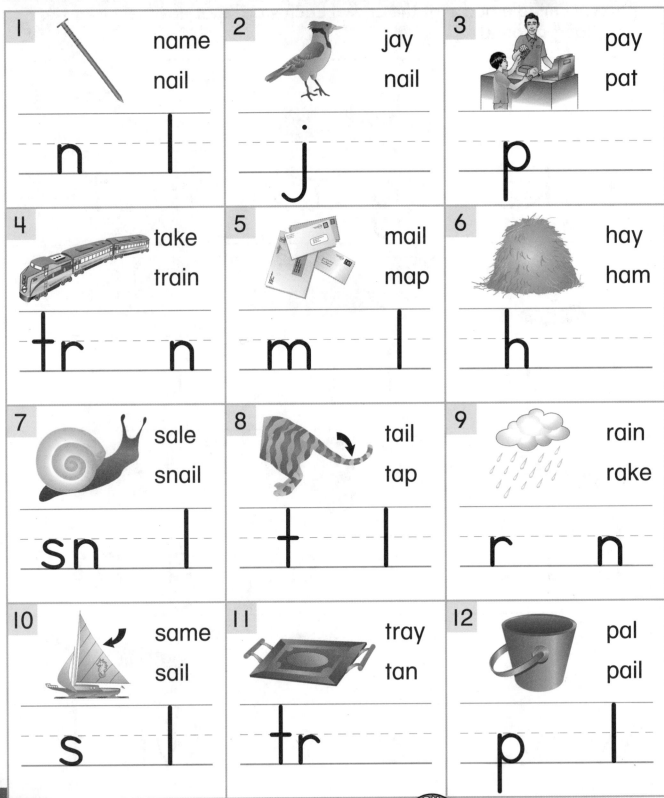

1. name
   nail
   n __ai__ l

2. jay
   nail
   j __ay__

3. **pay**
   pat
   p __ay__

4. take
   train
   tr __ai__ n

5. **mail**
   map
   m __ai__ l

6. **hay**
   ham
   h __ay__

7. sale
   snail
   sn __ai__ l

8. **tail**
   tap
   t __ai__ l

9. **rain**
   rake
   r __ai__ n

10. same
    sail
    s __ai__ l

11. **tray**
    tan
    tr __ay__

12. pal
    pail
    p __ai__ l

LESSON 86: Connecting Sound to Symbol: /ā/ai and ay

Read the long **a** words aloud. Then help your child write the words in two columns under the headings **ai** and **ay**.

Say the name of each picture. In each row, circle two pictures that have rhyming names. Then make a new rhyming word. Check your answers by saying the rhyming words with a partner.

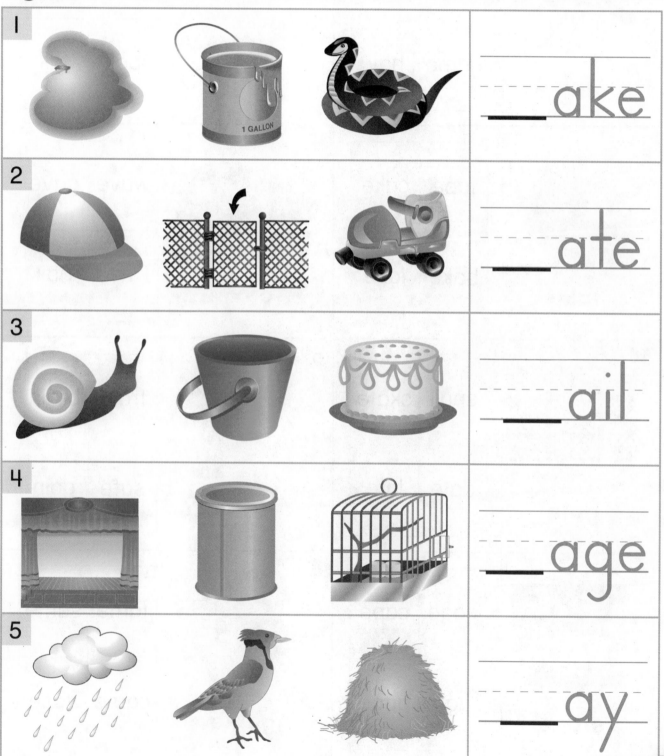

1. ____ake

2. ____ate

3. ____ail

4. ____age

5. ____ay

ay the name of each picture. Color each box that has a word that rhymes with the picture name.

1

jay

day	say
game	hay

2

sail

mail	vase
pail	tail

3

lake

tape	cake
bake	take

4

cave

wave	gave
Dave	nail

5

gate

snail	skate
date	late

6

rain

train	brain
safe	gain

7

stage

cage	cape
age	page

8

game

tame	same
came	vase

LESSON 87: Long Vowel **a** Phonograms

Help your child cut apart the word squares. Then mix them up and match the rhyming words together.

Say each word part. Say the name of each picture. Print the word on the line. Then add your own rhyming word and picture.

_ay	_ake	_ail
1	4	7
2	5	8
3	6	9

LESSON 88: Word Building with Long Vowel **a** Phonograms

173

1	2	3
ran rain rail	frame from fan	cake can cage
4	5	6
will whale wait	hay hat hill	safe same sat
7	8	9
plate late pat	stage stain age	rock ram rake
10	11	12
tape tap tip	top train tan	jet pay jay
13	14	15
saw sell sail	tray trap trip	can cane cot

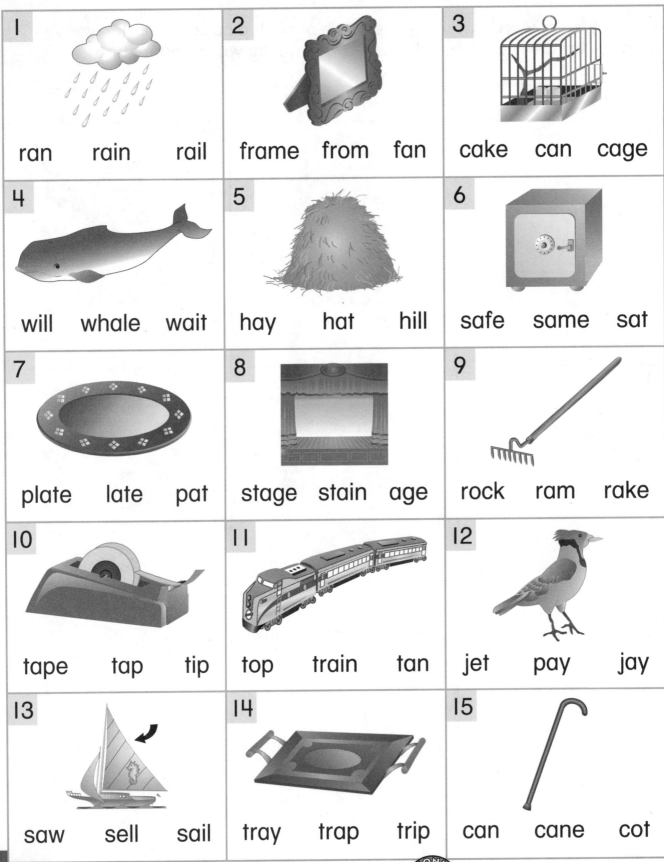

Read aloud all of the words on the page.
Let your child shout "Hooray!" after each
long a word.

Work Together

Say the name of each picture with a partner. Then circle the word and print it on the line.

1	lamp lake late	2	take tell tail	3	wait well wave
4	sell sail same	5	jay jet jam	6	game gum gate
7	name nail net	8	vane van vase	9	man make mail

Write a sentence about one picture using a long **a** word.

Read the name of each picture. Circle **L** if the name has the sound of long **a**. Circle **S** if the name has the sound of short **a**.

1 cape — L S	2 cap — L S
3 pay — L S	4 bat — L S
5 sail — L S	6 cane — L S
7 lake — L S	8 can — L S
9 jay — L S	10 pan — L S
11 hat — L S	12 rain — L S
13 hay — L S	14 bag — L S
15 jacks — L S	16 gate — L S

LESSON 89: Discriminating Between Long **a** and Short **a**

PHONICS Alive at Home

Randomly point to the pictures. Have your child **wave** for long **a** words and **snap** for short **a** words.

Your child has read this book in school. Ask him or her to read it to you. Then take turns finding all of the long **a** words in the story.

Name _____

Game Day Box

Fold

8   Will you make up a game?

I will take this box.   1

Fold

6   I will sail on the lake.

I will make a cave.   3

Directions: Cut and fold the book. Then read the story. Tell how the boy makes the box look different for each game.

LESSON 90: Long Vowel **a** Decodable Reader
Comprehension: Comparing and Contrasting

177

2 **It will be my game day box.**

I will bake a cake. 7

4 **I will make a safe.**

I will make a box for mail. 5

178 **LESSON 90:** Long Vowel **a** Decodable Reader
Comprehension: Comparing and Contrasting

Look at each picture. Circle the word that completes the sentence. Then print it on the line.

1	Don't _____ paper scraps.	win wet waste
2	Take an old picture _____.	frame from flat
3	_____ scraps onto it.	Pass Pat Paste
4	Draw your _____.	face fan fin
5	_____ it in the frame.	Tap Tape Tip
6	Hang it in a good _____.	place pal plate

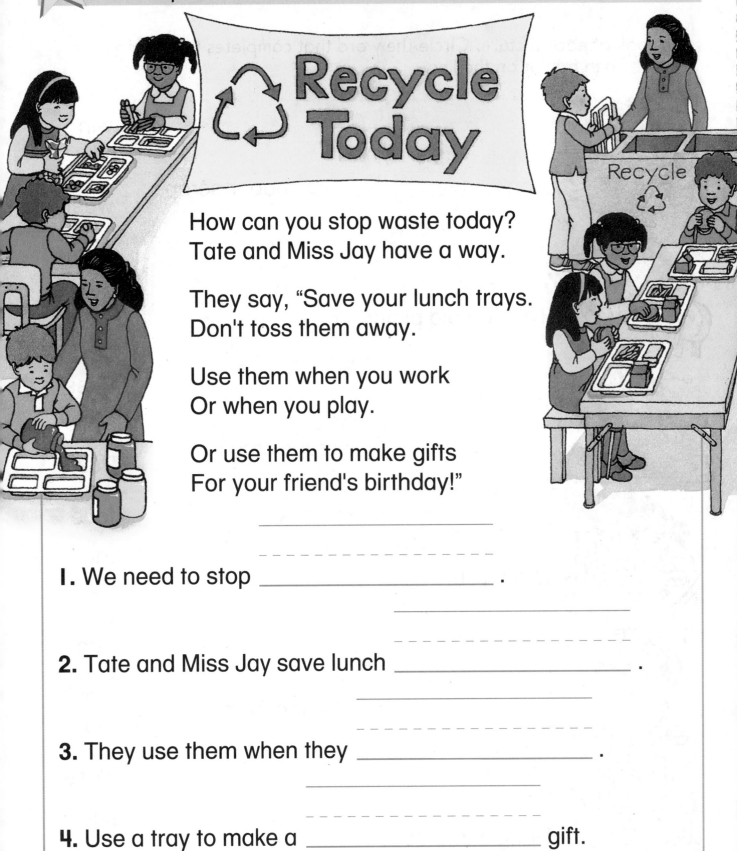

Recycle Today

How can you stop waste today?
Tate and Miss Jay have a way.

They say, "Save your lunch trays.
Don't toss them away.

Use them when you work
Or when you play.

Or use them to make gifts
For your friend's birthday!"

1. We need to stop _____ .

2. Tate and Miss Jay save lunch _____ .

3. They use them when they _____ .

4. Use a tray to make a _____ gift.

LESSON 91: Long Vowel **a** in Context
Comprehension: Identifying Problem/Solution

Help your child read labels on cans of food you have at home. Talk about any long **a** words you find.

In each game, score a tic-tac-toe by drawing a line through three pictures that have names with the sound of long **a.** Print the letters that stand for the long **a** sound in each game on the whale.

Say the name of each picture. If the picture name has the long **a** sound, find the letters in the box to complete the word. Print the letters on the line.

| a_e | ai | ay |

1 l ___ k

2 b ___ t

3 g ___ t

4 d ___ g

5 p ___

6 s ___ l

7 h ___

8 v ___ s

9 m ___ n

10 r ___ n

11 l ___ d

12 t ___ p

Review this Check-Up with your child.

Listen Listen as the page is read aloud. Talk about the long **i** words you hear, such as **five** and **vine.** Then circle the five bees.

Five in the Hive

Five bees wake up.
They leave the **hive**.
They see a **vine**,
And down they **dive**.

I **like** bees.
They're very **wise**.
Bees do **fine** work
For their small **size**.

Critical Thinking

What kind of work do bees do?

ive has the long **i** sound. Circle and color each picture that has the long **i** sound in its name.

LESSON 93: Phonemic Awareness: /ī/

Have your child say **hive** before each picture name (**hive/nine**) and tell if the vowel sounds are the same.

kite

The letters **i_e** can stand for the long **i** sound. The letter **e** is silent. Say each picture name. Then print **i** in the middle and **e** at the end of each word that has the long **i** sound.

1	2	3
b k	c v	l m

4	5	6
l d	r d	b t

7	8	9
h d	d m	p n

10	11	12
v n	h v	n n

LESSON 94: Connecting Sound to Symbol: /ī/ i_e

185

The letters **igh** and **ie** stand for the long **i** sound.

night   p<u>ie</u>

Say the name of each picture. Circle the word. Then print **igh** or **ie** on the line.

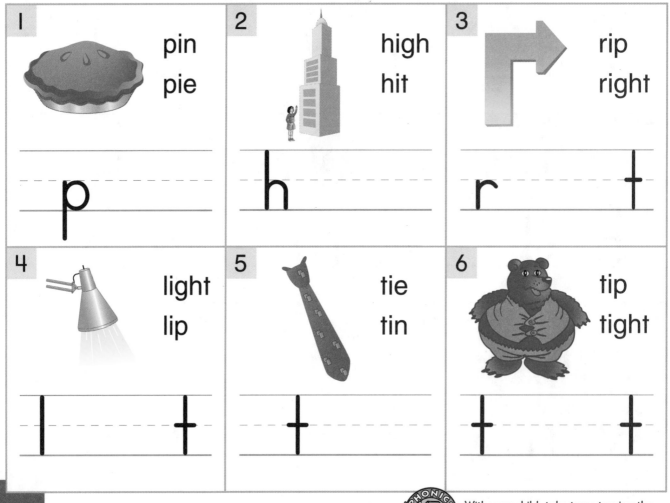

1	pin pie	p___
2	high hit	h___
3	rip right	r___t
4	light lip	l___t
5	tie tin	___t
6	tip tight	t___t

LESSON 95: Connecting Sound to Symbol: /ī/ **igh** and **ie**

With your child, take turns tracing the letters that stand for the long **i** sound in each word.

Say the name of each picture. In each row, circle two pictures that have rhyming names. Then make a new rhyming word. Check your answers with a partner's. Are they the same or different?

1				___ive
2				___ide
3				___ine
4				___ight

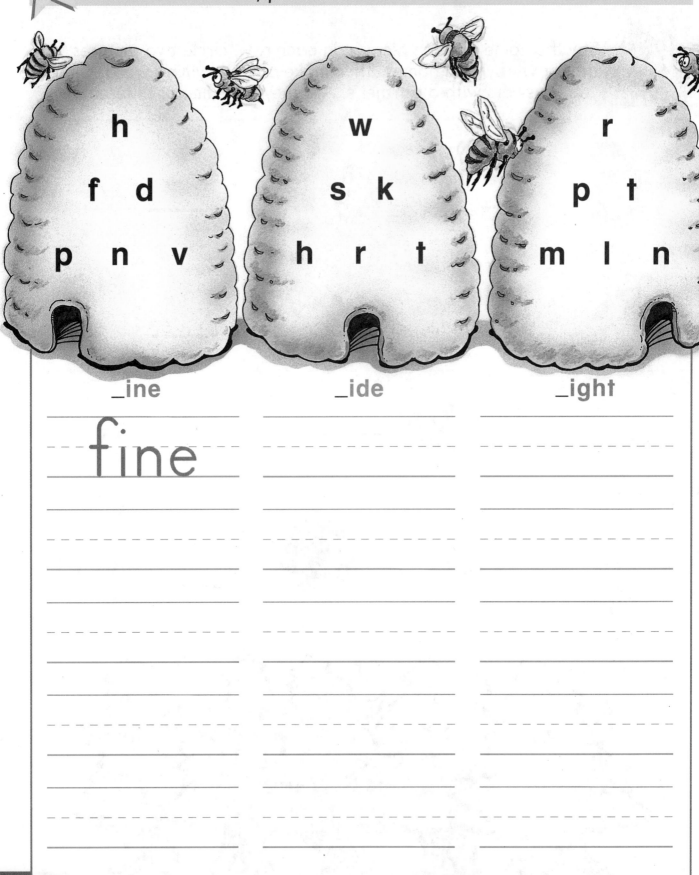

h
f   d
p   n   v

_ine

fine

w
s   k
h   r   t

_ide

r
p   t
m   l   n

_ight

With your child, build words by adding
letters to **_ime** and **_ile.**

Circle the word that names each picture.

| 1 | net   nine   nail | 2 | pin   pine   pen | 3 | bait   bit   bite |

| 4 | hide   had   high | 5 | brain   brick   bride | 6 | ripe   rain   rip |

| 7 | fire   fin   fan | 8 | kite   kit   kiss | 9 | tip   tape   tie |

| 10 | nip   night   nail | 11 | mine   men   man | 12 | slide   slid   slip |

| 13 | tape   tap   tight | 14 | bake   big   bike | 15 | pie   pay   pit |

Use the picture clues and words in the box to complete the puzzle. Print one letter in each box. Then write a sentence about one picture using a long **i** word.

hive	night	vine	tie	nine

ACROSS

1 

4 

DOWN

1 

2 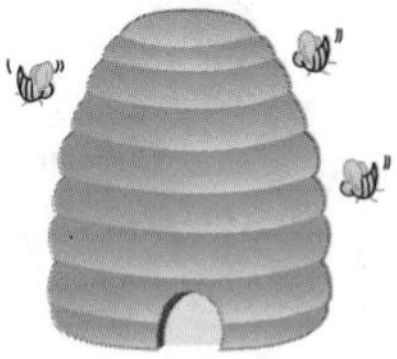

3 

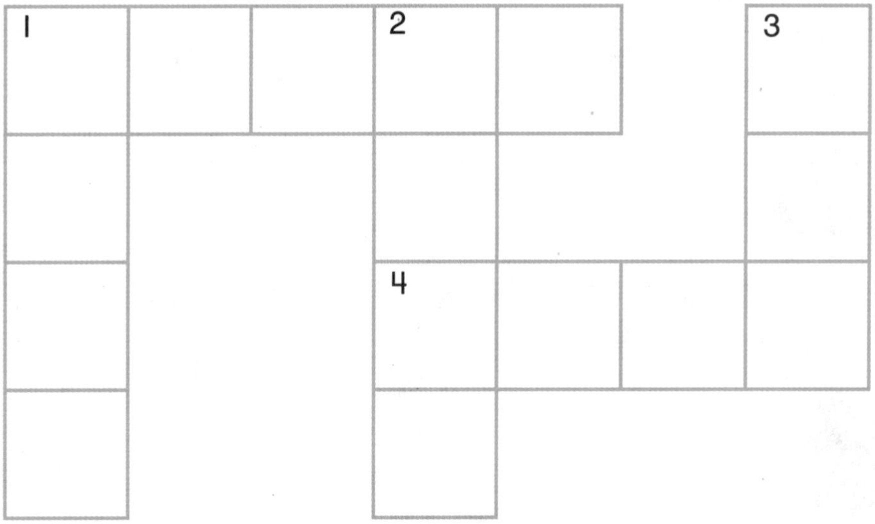

Have your child name each picture clue and point to the word in the puzzle.

Work Together

Say the name of each picture. Print the word on the line.
Then check your answers with a partner.

1	2	3

4	5	6

7	8	9

10	11	12
_____		

LESSON 98: Writing Long Vowel **i**

191

Long **i**

Short **i**

Help your child turn these short **i** words into long **i** words: **bit, fin, rip, hid**. Have your child write the long **i** words you make.

 I Can Read

Your child has read this book in school. Ask him or her to read it to you. Then have him or her find, read, and spell all of the long **i** words.

Name _____

A Fine Sale

Fold

Mike and Jen let Dad make the pie!

8

It is time for the sale.

1

Mike and Jen make a kite.

6

Fold

Mike and Jen get a tire.

3

Directions: Cut and fold the book. Then read the story. Tell how you think Mike and Jen made each thing.

 I Can Read

LESSON 99: Long Vowel **i** Decodable Reader
Comprehension: Drawing Conclusions

193

Mike and Jen dig in
a big pile.

2

Mike and Jen make
a fine ride.

7

Mike and Jen get a mop
and a tie.

4

Mike and Jen get a pie tin.

5

LESSON 99: Long Vowel i Decodable Reader
Comprehension: Drawing Conclusions

1		It is a _____ day.	fine fin fail
2		We _____ to Pine Lake.	ride red rake
3	PINE LAKE	It is on the _____ .	rate rig right
4		We _____ and swim.	high hike him
5	RECYCLE	Mom makes a _____ .	fan fill fire
6		It is _____ to go!	tail tie time

195

I Like the Earth

Day and night,
I like the earth.
I like tall pines,
And buds that smile
On leafy vines,
And fine, clear lakes
Where I can dive,
And bees that buzz
Inside their hive.

_____
- - - - - - - - - - -

1. Tall _____ are nice.

_____
- - - - - - - - - - -

2. Buds can grow on _____.

_____
- - - - - - - - - - -

3. It's fun to _____ right in to lakes.

_____
- - - - - - - - - - -

4. Bees buzz inside a _____.

LESSON 100: Long Vowel **i** in Context
Comprehension: Recognizing Main Idea and Details

Help your child draw a line under all of the long **i** words in the poem.

 **Check-Up**

Say the name of each picture. If the picture name has the long **i** sound, find the letters in the box to complete the word. Print the letters on the line.

i_e	igh	ie

1 p	2 h v	3 c p
4 n t	5 w g	6 l m
7 n n	8 s n	9 t
10 f n	11 r d	12 h

Print **a** or **i** in each empty box to make two words.
Read the words across and down.

1

```
    h
t [i] d  e
    d
    e
```

2

```
    g
t [ ] m  e
    m
    e
```

3

```
    p
c [ ] g  e
    g
    e
```

4

```
    b
k [ ] t  e
    t
    e
```

5

```
    h
b [ ] k  e
    k
    e
```

6

```
    s
p [ ] i  l
    i
    l
```

198 LESSON 101: Reviewing Long Vowels **a** and **i**

Listen Listen as the page is read aloud. Talk about the long **o** words you hear, such as **snow** and **coat**. Then draw a **nose, bow,** and **coat** on the snowman.

Let It Snow

I grab my **coat**
And out I **go**
To make a **snowman**
In the **snow**.

I'll **coast** down hills,
And make a fort.
A **snowy** day
Is much too short!

Critical Thinking

What should you wear to play in the snow?

LESSON 102: Phonemic Awareness: /ō/   199

Rose has the long **o** sound. Circle and color each picture that has the long **o** sound in its name.

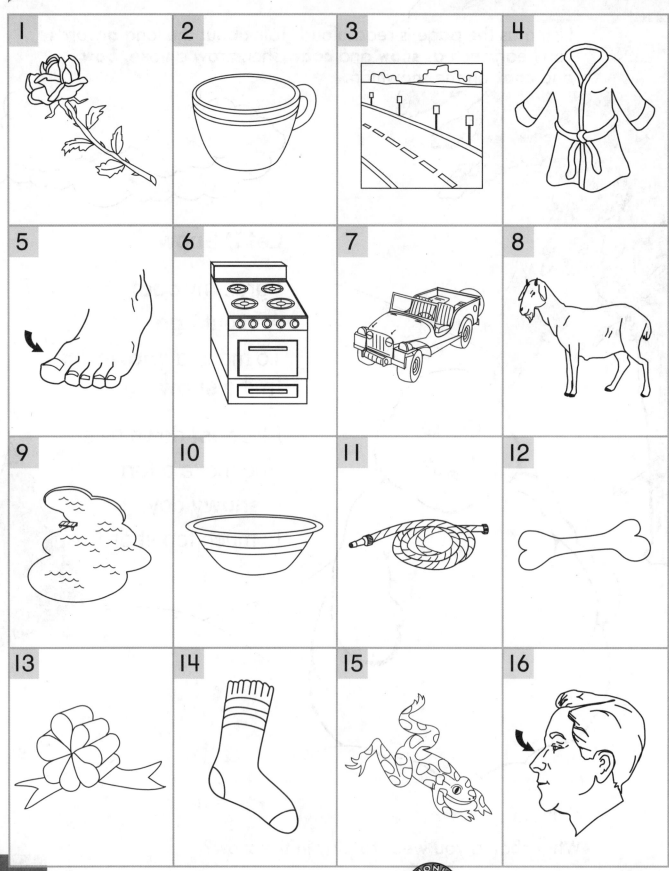

1	2	3	4
5	6	7	8
9	10	11	12
13	14	15	16

LESSON 102: Phonemic Awareness: /ō/

Name the pictures one at a time. Have your child point to his or her nose after every long **o** word.

The letters **o_e** can stand for the long **o** sound. The letter **e** is silent. Say the name of each picture. Then print **o** in the middle and **e** at the end of each word that has the long **o** sound.

c**o**n**e**

1 c _ n	**2** v _ s	**3** n _ t
4 r _ b	**5** b _ n	**6** d _ g
7 b _ n	**8** st _ v	**9** r _ p
10 h _ s	**11** d _ v	**12** sm _ k

LESSON 103: Connecting Sound to Symbol: /ō/ o_e

201

The letters **oa** and **ow** can stand for the long **o** sound. Say the name of each picture. Circle the word. Then print **oa** or **ow** on the line.

b**oa**t   sn**ow**

1	toad top	2	box bow	3	road rod
	t ___ d		b ___		r ___ d

4	row rob	5	goat got	6	bop bowl
	r ___		g ___ t		b ___ l

7	soap sob	8	mow mop	9	cot coat
	s ___ p		m ___		c ___ t

LESSON 104: Connecting Sound to Symbol: /ō/ **oa** and **ow**

Randomly read aloud the words on the page. Have your child stand on his or her tiptoes when he or she hears a long **o** word.

Help Joe recycle. Say the name of each picture. Color the newspapers that have pictures with rhyming names the same color.

1.

2.
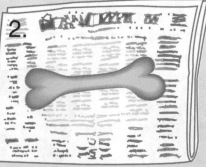

3.

4.

5.

6.

7.

8.

9.

10.
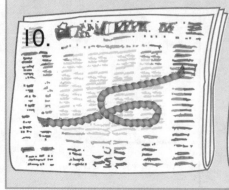

11.

12.

Say the name of each picture. In each row, circle two pictures that have rhyming names. Then make a new rhyming word.

1. ____ow

2. ____ose

3. ____oad

4. ____oat

Help your child use the new rhyming words in sentences.

Say each word part. Say the name of each picture. Print the word on the line. Then add your own rhyming word and picture. Work with a partner to make up more rhyming words.

_ose	_oat	_ow
1	4	7
2	5	8
3	6	9

1

snack   snail   snow

2

not   nail   note

3

cane   cone   can

4

sip   soap   sat

5

hike   hose   has

6

rope   rod   rip

7

bow   bad   bite

8

slate   stove   stop

9

tub   tide   toad

10

rot   raise   rose

11

smile   smoke   smell

12

coat   cot   kite

13

bite   bone   band

14

gate   get   goat

15

robe   rob   rib

Play Long o Charades. Take turns acting out and guessing each picture's name.

Work Together Say the name of each picture with a partner. Then circle the word and print it on the line.

1	soap sip safe	2	bake bite bone	3	bun bat bowl
4	ride road red	5	note night not	6	tie toe time
7	hole hat hill	8	net name nose	9	rip rope ripe

⭐ **W**rite a sentence about one picture using a long **o** word.

Read the name of each picture. Circle **L** if the name has the sound of long **o**. Circle **S** if the name has the sound of short **o**. Then color each picture that has the long **o** sound in its name.

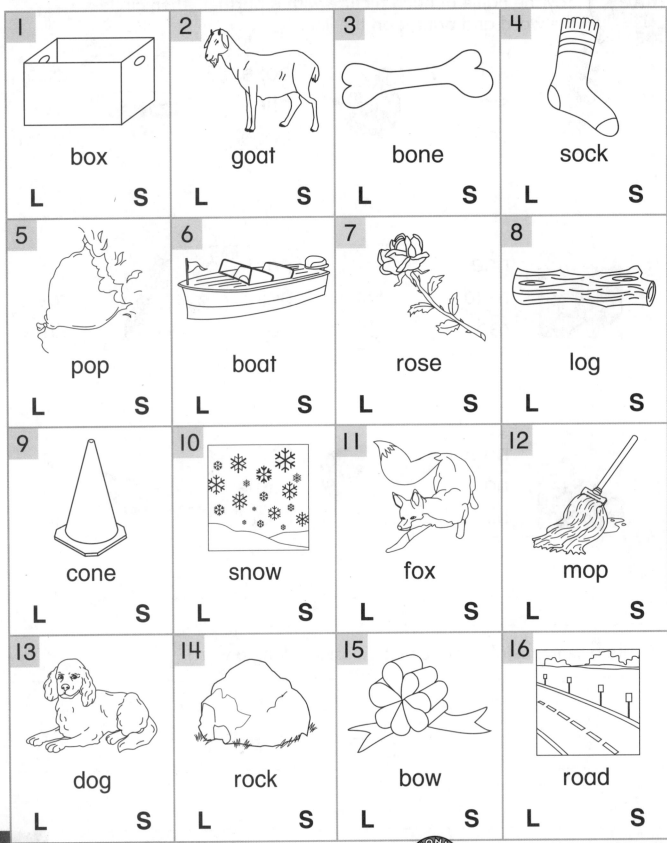

| 1 box | 2 goat | 3 bone | 4 sock |
| L   S | L   S | L   S | L   S |

| 5 pop | 6 boat | 7 rose | 8 log |
| L   S | L   S | L   S | L   S |

| 9 cone | 10 snow | 11 fox | 12 mop |
| L   S | L   S | L   S | L   S |

| 13 dog | 14 rock | 15 bow | 16 road |
| L   S | L   S | L   S | L   S |

LESSON 107: Discriminating Between
Long **o** and Short **o**

Have your child color the vowels in each word yellow. Help him or her recognize that short **o** words have only one vowel.

This home is fun for Joan
8 and the toad!

Your child has read this book in school. Ask him or her to read it to you. Then have him or her find at least one long **o** word on each page of the story.

Name _____

Joan and the Toad

Joan can row the boat.

1

The toad will jump in the lake.

6

Joan can see a mess.

3

Directions: Cut and fold the book. Then read the story. Tell why Joan needed to help the toad.

  LESSON 108: Long Vowel **o** Decodable Reader
Comprehension: Understanding
Cause and Effect

209

Joan can see a toad.

2

Joan will jump in the lake.

7

Can Joan save the home
for the toad?

4

Joan can help with a bag
and a pole.

5

LESSON 108: Long Vowel o Decodable Reader
Comprehension: Understanding Cause and Effect

Look at each picture. Circle the word that completes the sentence. Print it on the line. Then take turns reading the sentences with a partner.

1 Look at the _____.

snip
snake
snow

2 It is _____ white at first.

so
say
sock

3 There is dirt on the _____.

rope
rake
road

4 It is from _____.

smile
smoke
smell

5 Snow _____ up dirt.

soaps
soaks
sacks

6 Our _____ do, too!

cots
cast
coats

Tadpole to Toad

My tadpole floats in its home.
Its home is a big bowl.
The bowl has stones,
pond water, plants, and mud.

Is my tadpole a fish? No!
It will grow to be a toad.
I hope it grows up soon!
Then I'll let it go.

1. A tadpole can live in a _____.

2. A tadpole swims and _____.

3. A tadpole will grow to be a _____.

4. Will a fish grow up to be a toad? _____!

LESSON 109: Long Vowel **o** in Context
Comprehension: Comparing and Contrasting

Have your child find long **o** words in the story with these spellings: **o_e, oa, ow,** and **o.**

Say the name of each picture. If the picture name has the long **o** sound, find the letters in the box to complete the word. Print the letters on the line.

o_e	oa	ow

1

r ___ p

2

k ___ t

3

b ___ l

4

w ___ v

5

t ___ d

6

h ___ s

7

c ___ n

8

p ___ t

9

s ___ p

10

p ___ p

11

n ___ t

12

m ___

Read the words in the boxes. Combine words from boxes 1, 2, and 3 to make sentences. Print them on the lines. Then go back and underline the long vowel words in the sentences.

1	2	3
Kate and Jay	hike	to the lake.
Joan and Mike	race	down the road.
Five men	rode	to the right.

Help your child make up endings to these sentences: Mike likes to ____. Mrs. Dole bakes ____.

 **Check-Up**

Say the name of each picture. Circle the word and print it on the line.

1 tip / tape / tap	**2** cane / can / cone	**3** name / nine / note
4 road / rod / ride	**5** joke / jam / jay	**6** box / bow / bike
7 tag / tile / tail	**8** night / not / nail	**9** wave / wove / wait
10 rob / robe / rib	**11** time / tie / top	**12** high / hit / hope

LESSON 111: Assessing Long Vowels **a, i, o**   **215**

Say the name of each picture. Circle the word and print it on the line.

1	lit light late	2	note not night	3	like lab lake

4	hose hole hive	5	pail pie pole	6	cap cope cape

7	mole mail mile	8	got gate goat	9	line lime lane

10	vane vine van	11	high hay ham	12	row road ray

Listen as the page is read aloud. Talk about the long **u** words, such as **blue** and **fruit.** Then tell one thing you like about June.

June

Bright **blue** skies,
Bathing **suits,**
Inner **tubes,**
Fresh, ripe **fruit,**

Sandy **dunes,**
Happy **tunes,**
Barbecues—
I love **June**!

Critical Thinking

How are people in the picture making the beach
a safe and clean place?

LESSON 112: Phonemic Awareness: /o͞o/

June has the long **u** sound. Circle and color each picture that has the long **u** sound in its name.

1	2	3	4
5	6	7	8
9	10	11	12

LESSON 112: Phonemic Awareness: /o͞o/ and /yo͞o/

Help your child cut apart the pictures. Take turns finding the ones with long **u** in their names.

The letters **u_e** can stand for the long **u** sound. The letter **e** is silent. Say the name of each picture. Then print **u** in the middle and **e** at the end of each word that has the long **u** sound.

t_u_b_e

1	2	3
t b	J n	b n
4	5	6
l k	t n	m l
7	8	9
c b	r s	d n
10	11	12
c p	f l t	f v

LESSON 113: Connecting Sound to Symbol:
/o͞o/ u_e and /yo͞o/ u_e

219

The letters **ui** and **ue** stand for the long **u** sound.

fr<u>ui</u>t   bl<u>ue</u>

Say the name of each picture. Circle the word. Then print **ui** or **ue** on the line.

1 bud blue	**2** suit sun	**3** gum glue
bl___	s___t	gl___
4 fruit fume	**5** juice June	**6** sub Sue
fr___t	j___ce	S___

LESSON 114: Long Vowel **u** Spelling Patterns:
ui and **ue**

First have your child point to and read all of the words with **ui**. Then have him or her do the same for the **ue** words.

Look at the calendar page. Color six pictures that have the long **u** sound in their names. Check your work with a partner to see if you colored the same pictures.

LESSON 115: Recognizing Long Vowel **u**

221

1 **fl**ute	cute	cut	cane
2 **c**ube	tape	tub	tube
3 **d**une	tone	tune	time
4 **fr**uit	suit	size	sun
5 **m**ule	rail	rule	run
6 **g**lue	plum	cub	blue

LESSON 115: Long Vowel **u** in Rhyming Words

Let your child choose two rhyming words. Work together to use them in a short, silly poem.

Work Together

Say each word part. Say the name of each picture. Print the word on the line. Then work with a partner to add your own rhyming words.

1	_une	2	_uit	3	_ube

4	_ue	5	_ute

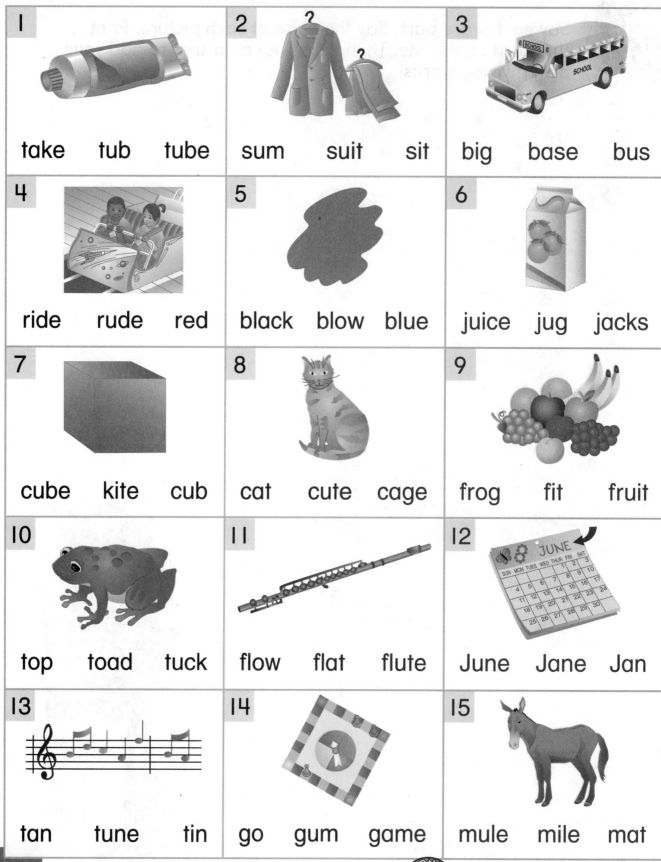

1 take   tub   tube

2 sum   suit   sit

3 big   base   bus

4 ride   rude   red

5 black   blow   blue

6 juice   jug   jacks

7 cube   kite   cub

8 cat   cute   cage

9 frog   fit   fruit

10 top   toad   tuck

11 flow   flat   flute

12 June   Jane   Jan

13 tan   tune   tin

14 go   gum   game

15 mule   mile   mat

Read aloud the long **u** words one at a time. Have your child orally spell each word.

Circle the name of the picture and print it on the line.

1 mile / mule / mail	2 tame / tab / tune	3 cube / code / cut
4 black / bud / blue	5 fruit / fat / fun	6 tape / tube / time
7 sit / sun / suit	8 just / juice / jail	9 date / dime / dune

Write a sentence about one picture using a long **u** word.

Say the name of each picture. If the word has the sound of long **u**, print it under the long **u** tube. If the word has the sound of short **u**, print it under the short **u** tube.

Long **u**

Short **u**

LESSON 117: Discriminating Between
Long **u** and Short **u**

PHONICS
Alive at Home

Print **tub, cut,** and **cub.** Have
your child add **e** to the end of
each word to make a new word.

Sue will help Duke.

8

Name _____

A Pet Mule

In June, Sue got a pet mule.

I

Do not run and be rude!

6

Sue made a cute suit for Duke.

3

Directions: Cut and fold the book. Then read the story. Tell whether or not you think this story can really happen.

LESSON 118: Long Vowel **u** Decodable Reader
Comprehension: Distinguishing Fantasy/Reality

227

Sue gave him a name.

2

Duke will help Sue.

7

Duke ran and made
a mess.

4

Sue made up a rule
for Duke.

5

Work Together

Look at each picture. Circle the word that completes the sentence. Print it on the line. Then explain to a partner how to make a cardboard flute.

1	Sue will make a _____ .	fun flute flat
2	She will use a _____ .	tub tape tube
3	She will paint it _____ .	blow blue bug
4	Luke will bring his _____ .	tuba tag tug
5	June will _____ an old box.	use us as
6	They will play a _____ .	toad tan tune

What Am I?

I have blue skies,
huge seas,
lively beasts,
ripe fruit,
soft winds that sound
like flutes,
and beauty everywhere.

Rude people pollute me.
My true friends salute me.
What am I?

1. Earth's friends like _____ skies.

2. Earth's friends like ripe _____.

3. Earth's friends do not _____.

4. Earth's true friends _____ it.

LESSON 119: Long Vowel **u** in Context
Comprehension: Recalling Details

Say the name of each picture. If the picture name has the long **u** sound, find the letters in the box to complete the word. Print the letters on the line.

u_e	ui	ue

1	2	3
t __ n	g l __	j __ g

4	5	6
c __ b	r __ w	s __ t

7	8	9
b l __	d __ n	l __ t

10	11	12
c __ p	f r __ t	m __ l

Unscramble the words to make a sentence. Print the sentence on the line. Then go back and circle the long vowel words.

1   June. in nice is Earth

_____

- - - - - - - - - - - - - - - - -

_____

2   blue. sky is The

_____

- - - - - - - - - - - - - - - - -

_____

3   on logs. Toads play

_____

- - - - - - - - - - - - - - - - -

_____

4   There snow. no is

_____

- - - - - - - - - - - - - - - - -

_____

5   coats away. our We put

_____

- - - - - - - - - - - - - - - - -

_____

6   ride We bikes day. all

_____

- - - - - - - - - - - - - - - - -

_____

Have your child read the sentences to you. Then take turns finding the long a, i, o, and u words.

Listen Listen as the page is read aloud. Talk about the long **e** words you hear, such as **green** and **trees.** Then complete the picture by drawing a person or animal.

Green Trees

Green trees,
Green trees!
They give us wood
And things to **eat.**
Branches hold
Our swing's **seat.**
We think **trees**
Are really **neat!**

Critical Thinking

What things made from trees do you see in your classroom?

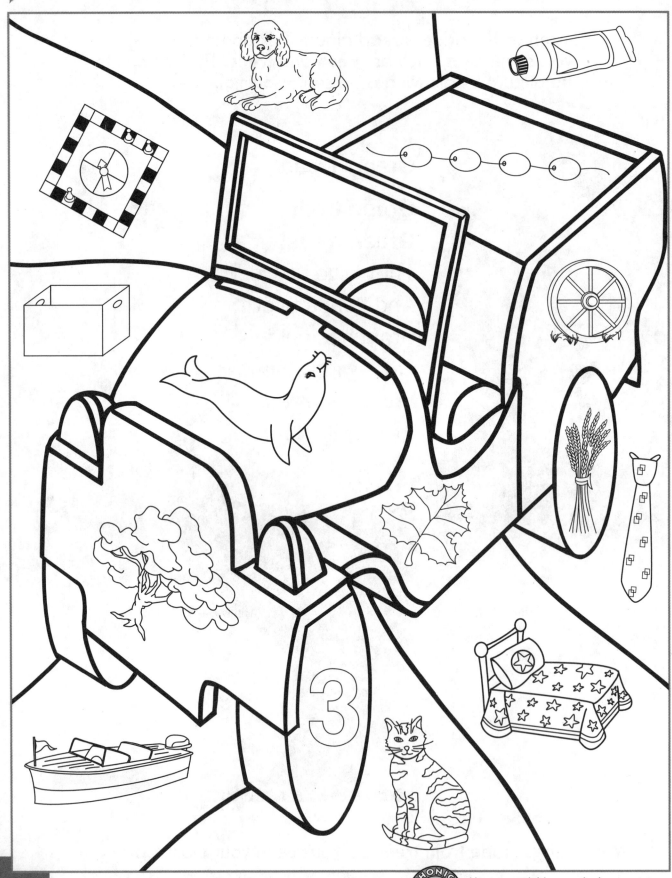

234   LESSON 121: Phonemic Awareness: /ē/

leaf

The letters **ea** can stand for the long **e** sound. Say the name of each picture. Print **ea** in the middle of each word that has the long **e** sound.

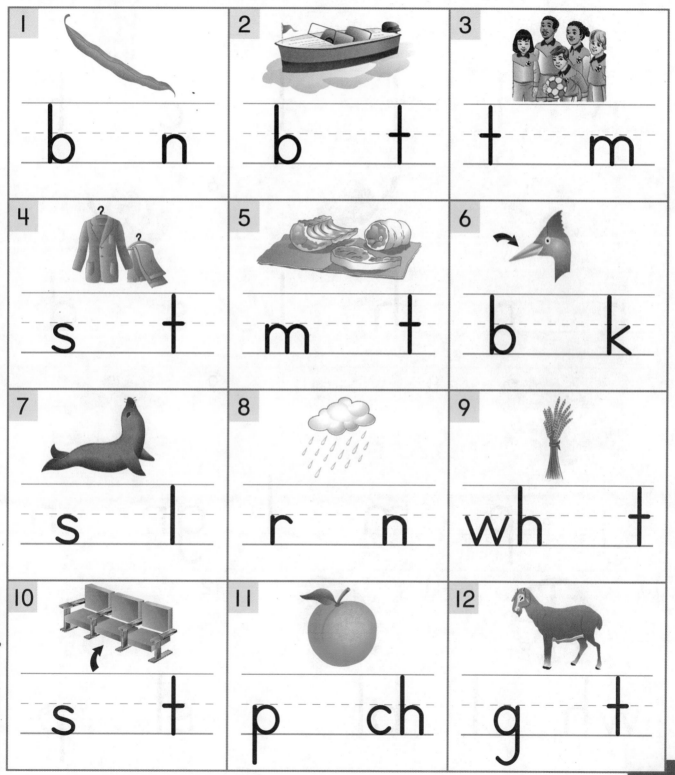

1	2	3
b ___ n	b ___ t	t ___ m
4	5	6
s ___ t	m ___ t	b ___ k
7	8	9
s ___ l	r ___ n	wh ___ t
10	11	12
s ___ t	p ___ ch	g ___ t

LESSON 122: Connecting Sound to Symbol: /ē/ **ea**

235

The letters **ee** can stand for the long **e** sound. Say the name of each picture. Print **ee** in the middle of each word that has the long **e** sound.

tree

1	2	3
p l	f t	c t
4	**5**	**6**
r n	h l	s d
7	**8**	**9**
j p	m l	gr n
10	**11**	**12**
wh l	bl	sl p

LESSON 123: Connecting Sound to Symbol: /ē/ ee

PHONICS Alive at Home

Write the letters **ee** five times on a sheet of paper. Have your child add letters to make new words.

Work Together

Work with a partner to find each pair of pictures that have rhyming names. Color their leaves the same color.

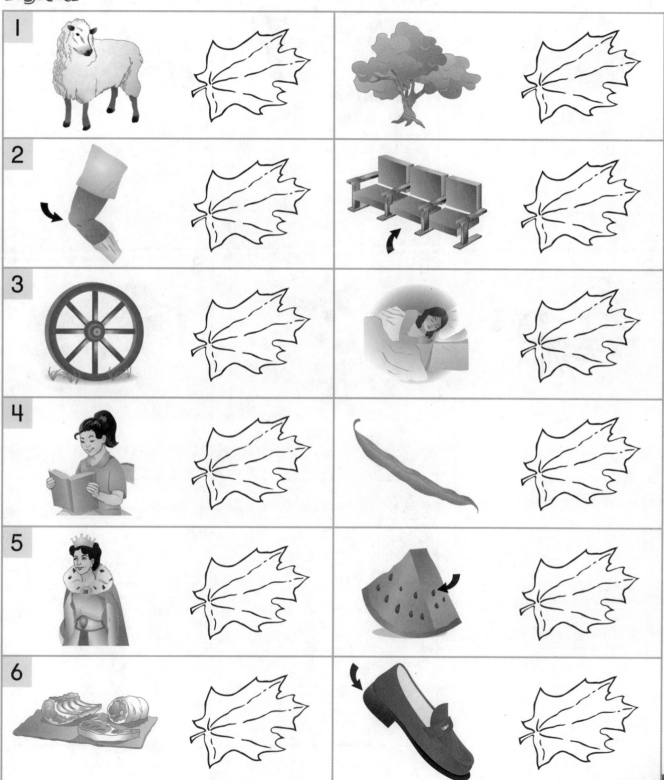

_ee	_eep	_eat
1	4	7
2	5	8
3	6	9

LESSON 124: Word Building with
Long Vowel e Phonograms

Read one of the words on the page. Have your child name words that rhyme with the word you read.

Work Together

Add each letter on the petal to the word part below it.
Say the word to a partner and print it on the line.

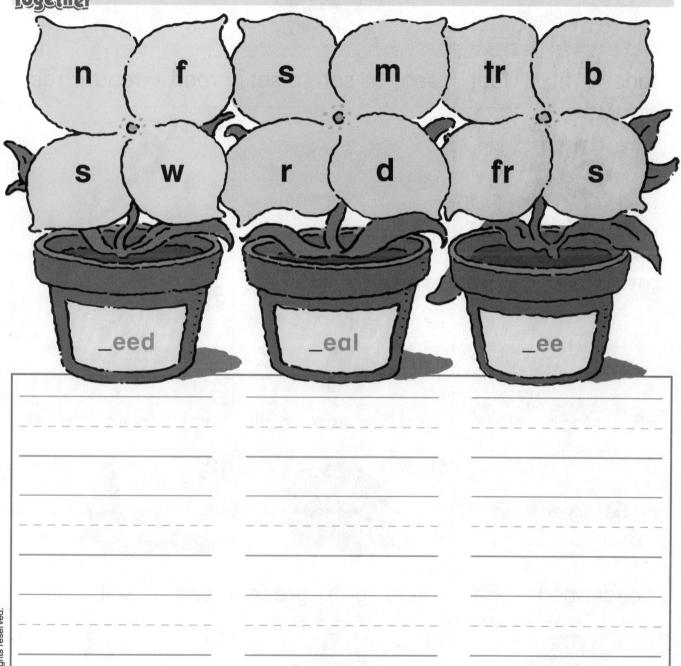

n   f   s   m   tr   b

s   w   r   d   fr   s

_eed   _eal   _ee

Circle the word that names each picture.

1. fade   fit   feet

2. seat   sat   set

3. road   read   red

4. loaf   leaf   life

5. mule   mat   meat

6. heel   hill   hole

7. slip   slope   sleep

8. quit   queen   quill

9. pail   pole   peel

10. beads   beds   bibs

11. grain   grin   green

12. seal   sail   sell

13. tree   trap   tray

14. side   sad   seed

15. bake   beak   bike

Randomly read the words on the page. Have your child tap his or her **feet** when he or she hears a long **e** word.

Say the name of each picture. Circle the word and print it on the line.

1		eat egg it	2		jet jump jeep	3		sale seal sell
4		tame time team	5		bow bee bay	6		mule mitt meat
7		true trip tree	8		read ride rude	9		pal peel pile

Write a sentence about one picture using a long **e** word.

Read the name of each picture. Circle **L** if the name has the sound of long **e**. Circle **S** if the name has the sound of short **e**. Then color each picture that has the long **e** sound in its name.

1 beads	2 bed	3 ten	4 meat
L S	L S	L S	L S
5 feet	6 beg	7 men	8 peas
L S	L S	L S	L S
9 desk	10 pet	11 beak	12 read
L S	L S	L S	L S
13 hen	14 bee	15 sled	16 team
L S	L S	L S	L S

242

LESSON 126: Discriminating Between
Long **e** and Short **e**

PHONICS Alive at Home

Ask your child to read the long **e** words, stretching out the long **e** sound like this: f-e-e-e-t.

8   Can you see a leaf yet?

Fold

Your child has read this book in school. Ask him or her to read it to you. Then have your child read and spell each long **e** word in the story.

I Can Read

Name _____

A Bean Seed

Take a bean seed.   I

6   Keep the seed wet.

Fold

Make a deep hole.   3

Directions: Cut and fold the book.
Then read the story. Tell how to
plant and take care of a bean seed.

I Can Read

LESSON 127: Long Vowel **e** Decodable Reader
Comprehension: Identifying Steps in a Process

243

2   Fill a pot with mud.

It will pop up.   7

4   Add the bean seed.

Set the pot in the sun.   5

LESSON 127: Long Vowel **e** Decodable Reader
Comprehension: Identifying Steps in a Process

Look at each picture. Circle the word that completes the sentence. Print it on the line. Then take turns reading the sentences with a partner.

1		Dee puts on her _____ .	jets jams jeans
2		Now she _____ a bag.	needs nods nails
3		She _____ Uncle Bob.	mats meets mitts
4		They go to the _____ .	bait bell beach
5		Each _____ they meet there.	week wet wake
6		They _____ up the beach.	clip clay clean

In the Big Tree

Last week Dad and I
saw a big tree.
Dad said, "Stay still, Lee.
Listen to the birds peep."

I looked up and saw
three baby birds in a nest.
Dad said, "Their mother will
bring them a nice meal."

_____

1. Last _____ we saw a big tree.

_____

2. We could hear the birds _____.

_____

3. _____ baby birds were in a nest.

_____

4. Their mother will bring them a _____.

LESSON 128: Long Vowel **e** in Context
Comprehension: Summarizing

With your child, name three things you can do together that have the long **e** sound in their names.

Check-Up

Say the name of each picture. If the picture name has the long **e** sound, find the letters in the box to complete the word. Print the letters on the line.

ea	ee

1	2	3
t ___ m	r ___ n	s ___ d

4	5	6
j ___	p ___ l	m ___ t

7	8	9
b ___ t	b ___ n	j ___ p

10	11	12
f ___ t	p ___	s ___ l

Read the sentences. First number the sentences in order to tell the story. Then print the sentences in order on the lines.

_____ Then, she gave it water.

_____ Next, she put a pine tree in it.

_____ She waits for it to grow.

_____ First, June made a hole.

1. _____

2. _____

3. _____

4. _____

LESSON 129: Reviewing Long Vowels **a, i, o, u, e**
Comprehension: Comparing and Contrasting

Have your child read the sentences. Ask him or her to point out words with long vowel sounds.

When **y** is at the end of a word, it can have the sound of long **i,** as in **sky,** or the sound of long **e,** as in **bunny.** Listen for the sounds of **y** in the rhyme.

sky   bunny

Up in the sky,
See the clouds fly by.
One looks like a bunny,
Isn't that funny?

Circle the picture if the **y** in its name has the long **i** sound. Draw a line under the picture if the **y** in its name has the long **e** sound.

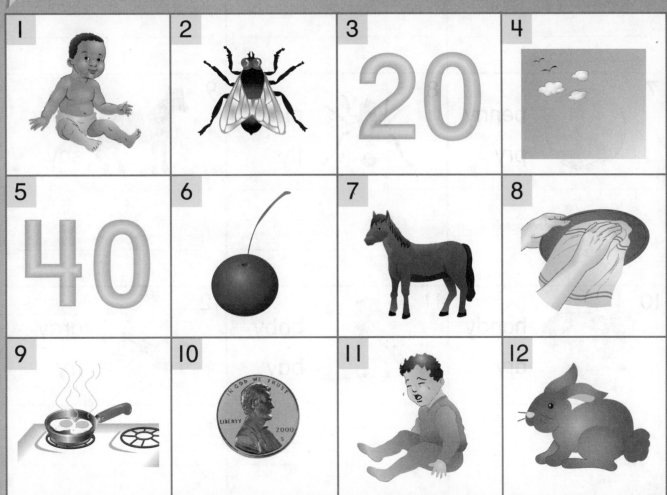

1	2	3	4
5	6	7	8
9	10	11	12

1 cherry
   cry
   _____
   - - - - - - - - - - -
   _____

2 daisy
   day
   _____
   - - - - - - - - - - -
   _____

3 buggy
   by
   _____
   - - - - - - - - - - -
   _____

4 **50** fifty
   fly
   _____
   - - - - - - - - - - -
   _____

5 candy
   cry
   _____
   - - - - - - - - - - -
   _____

6 silly
   sky
   _____
   - - - - - - - - - - -
   _____

7 penny
   pry
   _____
   - - - - - - - - - - -
   _____

8 play
   fly
   _____
   - - - - - - - - - - -
   _____

9 pony
   spy
   _____
   - - - - - - - - - - -
   _____

10 handy
    dry
   _____
   - - - - - - - - - - -
   _____

11 baby
    bay
   _____
   - - - - - - - - - - -
   _____

12 gray
    fry
   _____
   - - - - - - - - - - -
   _____

Count by tens to 100. Have your child repeat number words that end with the long **e** sound of **y,** such as **twenty.**

Read the name of each picture. Listen for the ending sound. Circle **i** if the **y** has the sound of long **i**. Circle **e** if the **y** has the sound of long **e**.

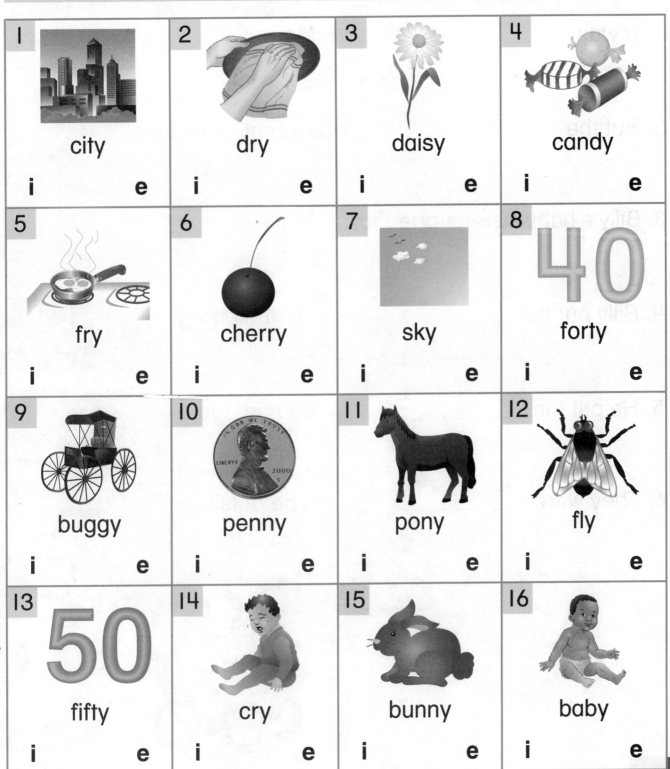

1 city — i e	2 dry — i e	3 daisy — i e	4 candy — i e
5 fry — i e	6 cherry — i e	7 sky — i e	8 forty — i e
9 buggy — i e	10 penny — i e	11 pony — i e	12 fly — i e
13 fifty — i e	14 cry — i e	15 bunny — i e	16 baby — i e

LESSON 131: Discriminating Between Final **y** as Long **e** and Long **i**

251

Listen as the page is read aloud. Use a word from the box to complete each sentence. Then print the word on the line.

fuzzy	sky	happy	windy	cry	baby

1. It was _____ outside.

2. But the _____ was sunny and blue.

3. Billy's baby sister started to _____.

4. Billy put the _____ in the buggy.

5. He put the _____ bear in, too.

6. They were_____ to be outside.

LESSON 131: Final **y** in Context
Comprehension: Identifying Problem/Solution

Talk about the weather. Help your child list and read weather words that end with **y**.

Say, spell, and talk about each word in the box. Then print each word under the vowel sound in its name.

like

use

gave

hose

jay

juice

keep

right

own

leaf

bunny

sky

Long a

1. gave

2.

Long u

7.

8.

Long i

3.

4.

Long e

9.

10.

Long o

5.

6.

y as Long i

11.

y as Long e

12.

LESSON 132: Connecting Spelling, Writing, and Speaking

253

Write to Jake and Lane and tell them how they can be kind to the Earth. Use one or more of your spelling words. Then talk about what you wrote.

like	gave	jay	keep	own	right
use	hose	juice	bunny	leaf	sky

To Jake: _____

_____

_____

_____

_____

To Lane: _____

_____

_____

_____

RECYCLE

LESSON 132: Connecting Spelling, Writing, and Speaking

PHONICS Alive at Home

With your child, think of one way your family can be kinder to the Earth. Use one of the spelling words in your idea.

Fill in the circle next to the name of each picture.

1	2	3
○ sail ○ seal ○ sell	○ glum ○ glue ○ glow	○ rate ○ right ○ rat

4	5	6
○ pile ○ pal ○ peel	**50** ○ fit ○ fat ○ fifty	○ gate ○ game ○ gum

7	8	9
○ tame ○ team ○ ten	○ suit ○ sit ○ seat	○ mile ○ mule ○ mail

10	11	12
○ high ○ heat ○ hay	○ rose ○ raise ○ rise	○ pea ○ pay ○ pie

13	14	15
○ cot ○ coat ○ cute	○ bike ○ beak ○ bake	○ bill ○ bail ○ bowl

LESSON 133: Assessing Long Vowels
a, i, o, u, e, and Final **y**

255

 **Check-Up** Fill in the circle next to the name of each picture.

1	2	3
○ bone ○ bean ○ bin	○ road ○ red ○ read	○ blue ○ blow ○ bite

4	5	6
○ free ○ fray ○ fry	○ wait ○ wave ○ wove	○ tip ○ tie ○ tea

7	8	9
○ fruit ○ right ○ free	○ road ○ row ○ ray	○ bay ○ bet ○ bee

10	11	12
○ rain ○ ran ○ rail	○ nut ○ neat ○ night	○ cube ○ cub ○ cob

13	14	15
○ seep ○ sap ○ soap	○ jet ○ jay ○ juice	○ him ○ cave ○ hive

LESSON 133: Assessing Long Vowels
a, i, o, u, e, and Final y

Review this Check-Up with your child.

Look and Learn

Listen as the page is read aloud. Look at the pictures. Then talk about what you see.

Earth is our home.
It gives us nice things
like pine trees, blue lakes,
fruit to eat, and green grass.
We must take care of Earth.
We must keep it safe and clean.

How are the people in the
pictures helping Earth?
How can you help Earth?

LESSON 134: Long Vowels in Context
Comprehension: Making Inferences

257

The words in the box are often used in sentences.
Use one of the words to complete each sentence.
Then practice reading the sentences aloud.

down	How	little	Please	Put	said

1. I said, "_____ help the sea ."

2. Keep the _____ safe.

3. Mom _____, "Please help the ."

4. Do not cut _____ .

5. _____ can you help save the ?

6. _____ that  in a bin.

Randomly point to the words in the
box and have your child read them.
Repeat this activity frequently.

Say the name of each picture. Circle the word. Then circle **L** if the name has a long vowel sound or **S** if the name has a short vowel sound.

1 cob cube cub **L** **S**	2 bike bake beak **L** **S**	3 mine mean men **L** **S**
4 goat get gate **L** **S**	5 bat bee bed **L** **S**	6 fine fun fin **L** **S**
7 top tape tap **L** **S**	8 skip soak sky **L** **S**	9 road rod read **L** **S**
10 sit seat suit **L** **S**	11 vane vine van **L** **S**	12 mile mule meal **L** **S**

Check-Up

Say the name of each picture. Circle **long** if the name has a long vowel sound or **short** if the name has a short vowel sound. Then print the name of the picture on the line.

1	long short	2	long short	3	long short
4	long short	5	long short	6	long short
7	long short	8	long short	9	long short
10	long short	11	long short	12	long short

Review this Check-Up with your child.

Ears Hear

Flies buzz,
Motors roar.
Kettles hiss,
People snore.
Dogs bark,
Birds cheep.
Autos honk: **Beep! Beep!**

Winds sigh,
Shoes squeak.
Trucks honk,
Floors creak.
Whistles toot,
Bells clang.
Doors slam: **Bang! Bang!**

Kids shout,
Clocks ding.
Babies cry,
Phones ring.
Balls bounce,
Spoons drop.
People scream: **Stop! Stop!**

Lucia and James L. Hymes, Jr.

Critical Thinking

Which sounds are loud? soft?
What sounds make you feel happy?

LESSON 137: Consonant Blends
Phonemic Awareness: Rhyme

Name _____

Dear Family,

In this unit about our five senses, your child will learn the sounds of consonant blends. As your child progresses through this unit, you can try these activities together at home.

• Say the name of each picture below with your child. Listen to the sounds of the consonant blends.

Apreciada Familia:

En esta unidad se enseñarán los cinco sentidos y los sonidos de dos consonantes juntas. Ustedes pueden hacer estas actividades juntos en la casa.

• Con su niño pronuncien los nombres de los objetos en los cuadros. Escuchen los sonidos de las consonantes al principio de la palabra.

l blend l principio	r blend r principio	s blend s principio	final blend final

clown	**fr**uit	**st**op	ba**nd**

• Read the poem "Ears Hear" on the reverse side of this page.

• Find words with consonant blends in the poem, such as **flies, snore, honk, trucks, clang, clocks, cry, ring, spoons, drop, scream,** and **stop.**

• Then find the rhyming words. (roar/snore, cheep/Beep, squeak/creak, clang/Bang, ding/ring, drop/Stop)

• Lea el poema "Ears Hear" en la página 261.

• Encuentren sonidos de dos consonantes juntas en el poema, tales como: **flies, snore, honk, trucks, clang, clocks, cry, ring, spoons, drop, scream** y **stop.**

• Después encuentren las palabras que riman. (roar/snore, cheep/Beep, squeak/creak, clang/Bang, ding/ring, drop/Stop)

PROJECT

Be very quiet, close your eyes for a short time, and listen carefully. Then make a list of sounds you heard in your home or outside. Also list the things that made the sounds. Circle any consonant blends you use.

tick   tick

tick   tick

PROYECTO

Rápido cierren los ojos por poco tiempo y escuchen con cuidado. Luego hagan una lista de los sonidos que escucharon afuera y en la casa. Hagan una lista de lo que hizo el sonido y encierren en un círculo cuando aparezcan dos consonantes juntas.

Play starts with the **l** blend **pl.** Listen for the sounds of **l** blends in the rhyme.

When I play ball, it's noisy.
I slide and the fans all clap.
But please be quiet now.
I'm going to take a nap.

In each row, circle and color each picture that has the same **l** blend at the beginning of its name as the picture in the box.

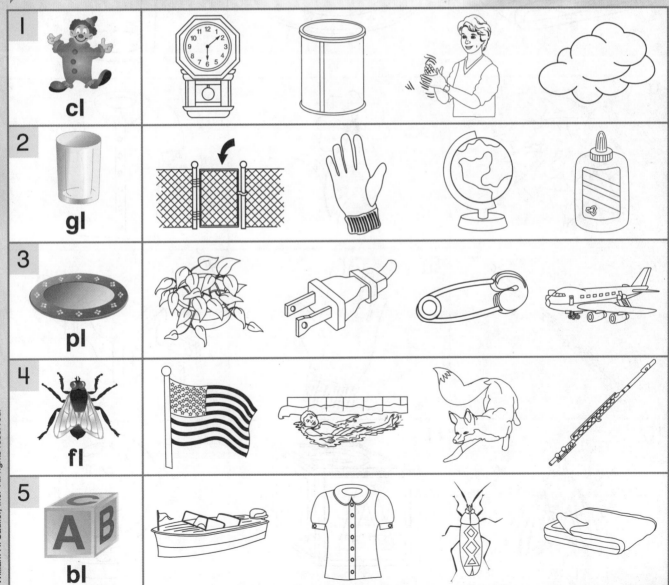

Blue, glue, plane, and **flag** begin with **l** blends. Color the pictures if their names begin with **bl** ✏️, **gl** ✏️, **pl** ✏️, **fl** ✏️.

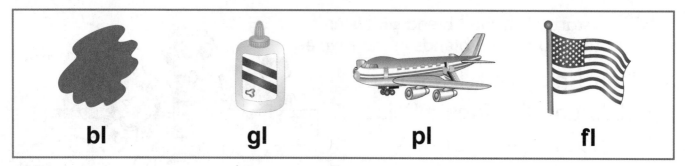

bl   **gl**   **pl**   **fl**

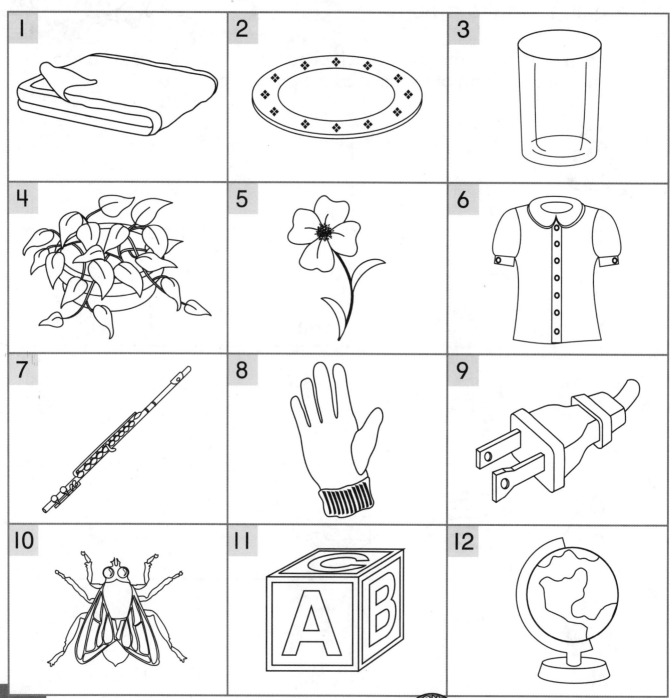

1 2 3

4 5 6

7 8 9

10 11 12

LESSON 138: Practicing l Blends

Help your child list things in your home that have names beginning with **l** blends, such as **floors** and **plants**.

Say the name of each picture with a partner. Then circle the word and print it on the line.

1	flat fit feet	2	bell bee blue	3	cape clap cap
4	back bake block	5	pine plane pan	6	flute fell fin
7	club cub cube	8	late pat plate	9	flag frog fig

Write a sentence about one picture using a word that begins with an l blend.

Our Senses

Hear the wind blow.
See the blue sky.
Hear the clock tick
And the loud, buzzing fly.

Feel the smooth glass.
Smell the sweet flower.
Hear the plane roar
As it flies by the tower.

1. What can you smell?

_____
_____
_____
_____

2. What can you feel?

_____
_____
_____
_____

266

Sit with your child and talk about what you hear, see, feel, smell, and taste. Write down any words that start with an **l** blend.

Dragon starts with the **r** blend **dr.** Listen for the sounds of **r** blends in the rhyme.

Watch the dragon fly.
Feel his wings brush by.
Try to ride him if you dare.
Friendly dragons never care.

In each row, circle and color each picture that has the same **r** blend at the beginning of its name as the picture in the box.

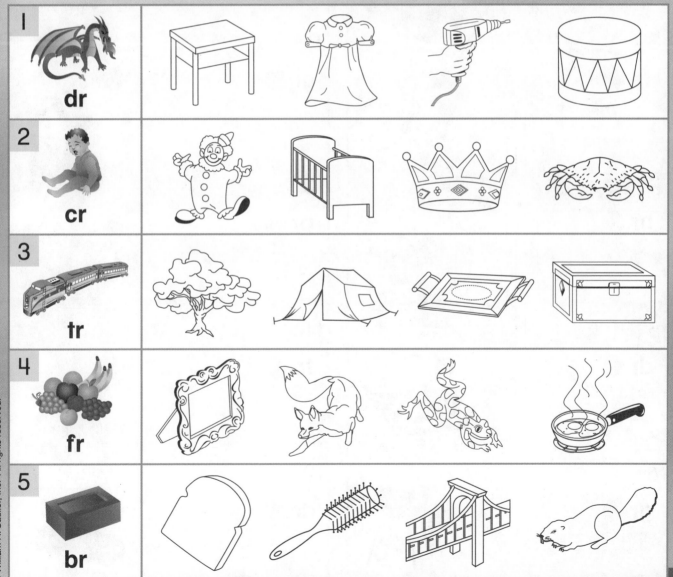

1 **dr**				
2 **cr**				
3 **tr**				
4 **fr**				
5 **br**				

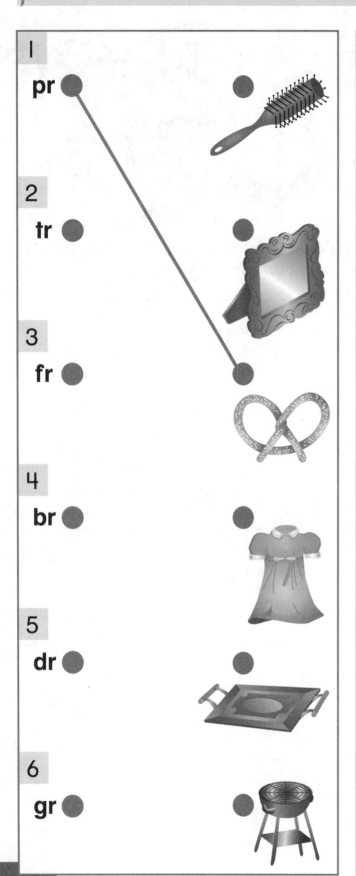

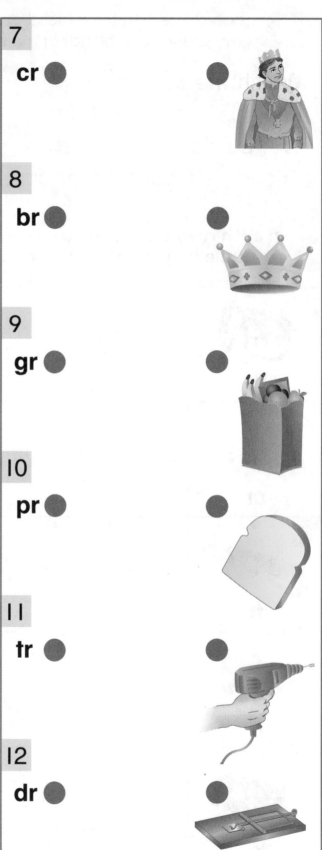

1 pr

2 tr

3 fr

4 br

5 dr

6 gr

7 cr

8 br

9 gr

10 pr

11 tr

12 dr

Work Together

Say the name of each picture with a partner. Then circle the word and print it on the line.

1	flag fog frog	2	prize plays pies	3	drop drum dime
4	club crab cab	5	bride ride brick	6	globe get green
7	rail drill drain	8	rain train tail	9	tie tire tree

Write a sentence about one picture using a word that begins with an **r** blend.

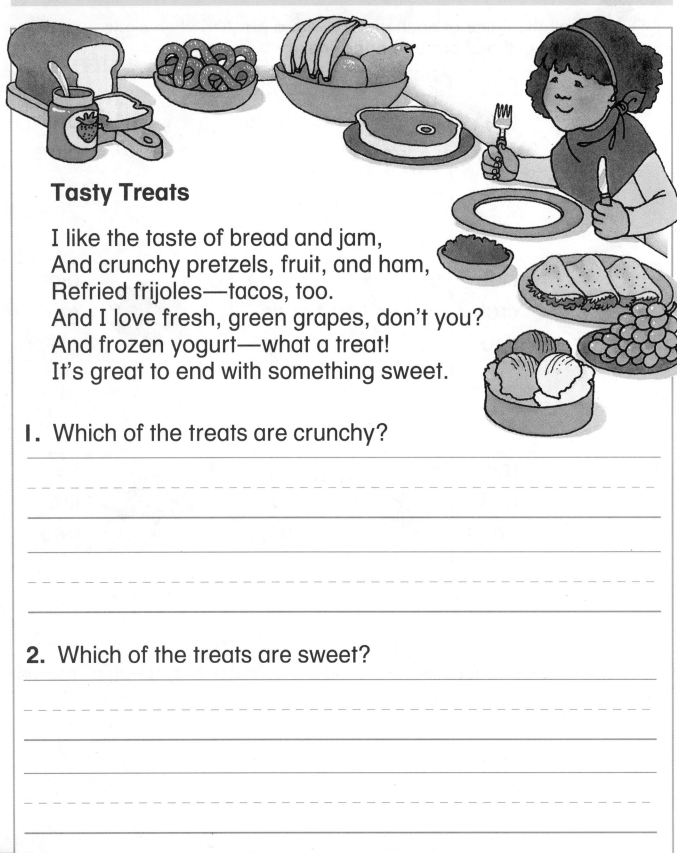

Tasty Treats

I like the taste of bread and jam,
And crunchy pretzels, fruit, and ham,
Refried frijoles—tacos, too.
And I love fresh, green grapes, don't you?
And frozen yogurt—what a treat!
It's great to end with something sweet.

1. Which of the treats are crunchy?

_____

- -

_____

_____

- -

2. Which of the treats are sweet?

_____

- -

_____

_____

- -

LESSON 141: Words with **r** Blends in Context
Comprehension: Classifying Objects

PHONICS
Alive at Home

Help your child make a list of healthy treats. Have him or her circle any words that begin with **r** blends.

Spaghetti starts with the **s** blend **sp.** Listen for the sounds of **s** blends in the rhyme.

I love spaghetti.
It's my special treat.
It's good when it's spicy,
And sloppy to eat.

Say the name of the pictures in each row. Circle the pictures with names that begin with the same **s** blend.

1.
st
sk
sl

2.
sm
sc
spr

3.
sp
sl
sn

4.
sn
sc
sw

5.
sl
sn
squ

6.
sm
sp
scr

7.
sk
st
sl

8.
sw
sn
sm

9.
sc
spr
st

10.
sn
spr
str

11.
scr
sp
sw

12.
str
squ
sp

Draw the outline of a large star.
Help your child write words that
begin with **s** blends inside the star.

Say the name of each picture with a partner. Then circle the word and print it on the line.

1 square star spare	**2** sting ring string	**3** swell spill seal
4 snail nail sail	**5** spy say sky	**6** slide side smile
7 wing swing sling	**8** spray say ray	**9** sell smell spell

Write a sentence about one picture using a word that begins with an **s** blend.

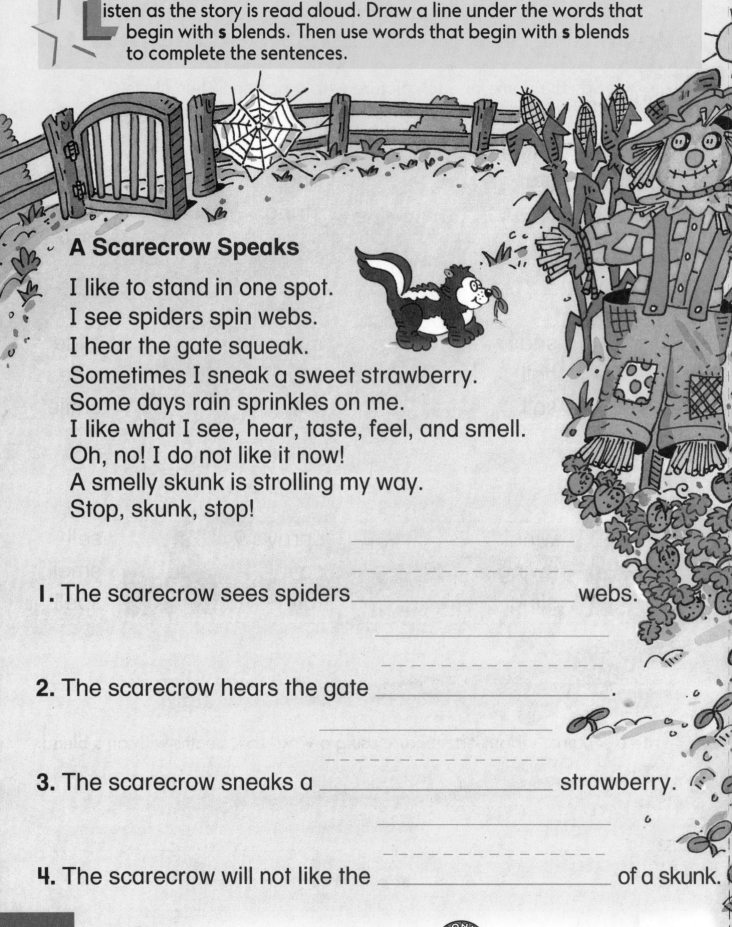

Listen as the story is read aloud. Draw a line under the words that begin with **s** blends. Then use words that begin with **s** blends to complete the sentences.

A Scarecrow Speaks

I like to stand in one spot.
I see spiders spin webs.
I hear the gate squeak.
Sometimes I sneak a sweet strawberry.
Some days rain sprinkles on me.
I like what I see, hear, taste, feel, and smell.
Oh, no! I do not like it now!
A smelly skunk is strolling my way.
Stop, skunk, stop!

1. The scarecrow sees spiders _____ webs.

2. The scarecrow hears the gate _____ .

3. The scarecrow sneaks a _____ strawberry.

4. The scarecrow will not like the _____ of a skunk.

LESSON 143: Words with **s** Blends in Context
Comprehension: Making Predictions

Have your child draw a picture of a scarecrow. Talk about the things you would use to make it.

Band ends with the blend **nd.** Ring ends with the blend **ng.** Other blends can end words, too. Listen for final blends in the rhyme.

Listen to the band.
Hear the music ring.
Give the band a hand.
Then join in and sing.

Say the name of each picture. Circle the letters that stand for the final blend in each picture name.

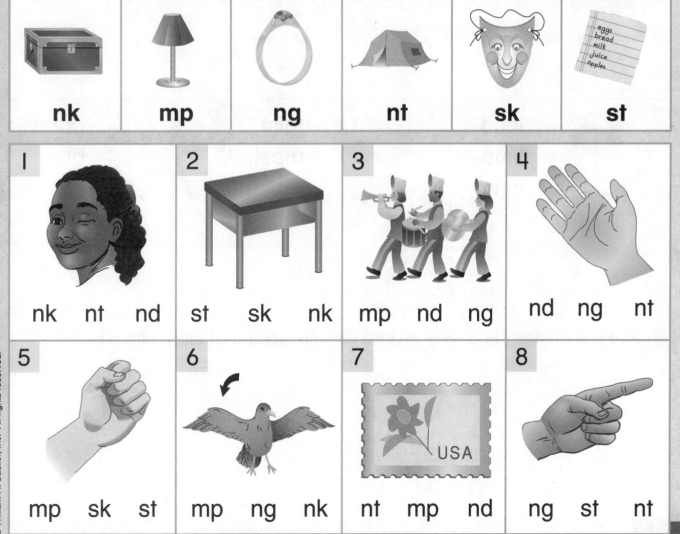

| nk | mp | ng | nt | sk | st |

1 nk nt nd   **2** st sk nk   **3** mp nd ng   **4** nd ng nt

5 mp sk st   **6** mp ng nk   **7** nt mp nd   **8** ng st nt

Say the name of each picture with a partner. Then circle the word and print it on the line.

1 hint / had / hand	2 kiss / king / cone	3 desk / dime / dent
4 win / wink / wig	5 tent / team / ten	6 let / list / lid
7 land / lime / lamp	8 mist / mask / make	9 band / bad / bat

Write a sentence about one picture using a word that ends with a blend.

Help your child write words that rhyme with some of the picture names. Circle the final blend in each word.

Say, spell, and talk about each word in the box.
Then print each word under the blend in its name.
Circle the letters that spell the blends.

small		
blue	**l Blends**	**s Blends**
grill	1 (bl)ue	7
sweet	2	8
dry	3	9
glad	**r Blends**	**Final Blends**
long	4	10
pretty	5	11
band	6	12
spin		
went		
clean		

Spell, Write, and Tell

Write a note to thank a friend for a great party. Use some of your spelling words. Then tell about what you wrote.

small	grill	dry	long	band	went
blue	sweet	glad	pretty	spin	clean

_____

- -

Dear _____ ,

_____

- -

_____

- -

_____

- -

_____

- -

_____

- -

_____

Your friend,

_____

- -

_____

LESSON 145: Connecting Spelling, Writing, and Speaking

Help your child write and mail or e-mail a note to a friend or relative.

Look and Learn

Listen as the page is read aloud. Look at the pictures.
Then talk about what you see.

Most people have five senses.
We can see, hear, smell,
taste, and feel. We use
our senses all the time.

Look at the pictures.
Do you see green and blue?
Pretend you are playing the game.
What sound does the crowd make?
Does the mitt feel smooth?
What can you smell?
Wouldn't some crunchy popcorn and
a cool drink taste good right now?

Using all your senses
is fun. Try it!

LESSON 146: Words with Consonant Blends in Context
Comprehension: Classifying Objects

The words in the box are often used in sentences. Use one of the words to complete each sentence. Then practice reading the sentences aloud.

| again | ate | big | Look | to | yellow |

1. Glen and Brad rode a bus _____ the _____ .

2. Brad said, "I see a _____ _____ ."

3. Glen said, "I see a _____ _____ ."

4. Glen said, "_____ at the _____ ."

5. Brad said, "I _____ a _____ ."

6. Glen and Brad will ride the bus _____ .

LESSON 147: Reading High-Frequency Words

Have your child find the word **yellow** in the box. Talk about things that are yellow.

Remember

Use the picture clues to fill in the puzzle.
Print one letter in each box.

ACROSS ➡️ 2   4   5

DOWN ⬇️

1

3

6

Check-Up Say the name of each picture. Print the letters that stand for the missing blend on the lines.

1 _____ ap	2 _____ ane	3 _____ ail
4 ha _____	5 _____ ee	6 la _____
7 _____ ar	8 de _____	9 _____ ag
10 _____ ide	11 li _____	12 _____ ide

Review this Check-Up with your child.

Read Aloud

CLOUDS

White sheep, white sheep
On a blue hill,
When the wind stops
You all stand still.
When the wind blows
You walk away slow.
White sheep, white sheep,
Where do you go?

Christina G. Rossetti

Critical Thinking

How would the clouds look on a stormy day?
What do the different kinds of clouds tell you about the weather?

LESSON 149: Consonant Digraphs
Phonemic Awareness: Initial Sounds

Name _____

Dear Family,

In this unit about weather, your child will learn the sounds of consonant digraphs. You can participate with your child by doing these home activities.

• Say the name of each picture below with your child. Listen to the sounds of the beginning consonant digraphs **th**, **sh**, **wh**, **ch**, and **kn**.

Apreciada Familia:

En esta unidad se hablará del tiempo y se enseñarán los sonidos dígrafos de las consonantes. Pueden practicarlos con su hijo haciendo estas actividades en la casa.

• Pronuncien el nombre de los objetos en los cuadros. Escuchen los sonidos dígrafos de las consonantes al principio de las palabras, **th**, **sh**, **wh**, **ch** y **kn**.

th	sh	wh	ch	kn
			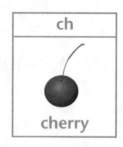	
thumb	sheep	whale	cherry	knot

• Read the poem "Clouds" on the reverse side of this page.

• Talk about the shapes of clouds you see in the sky. What do they remind you of?

• Help your child find words with consonant digraphs in the poem, such as **white**, **sheep**, **when**, and **where**. Then find the rhyming words. (hill/still, slow/go)

• Lean el poema "Clouds" en la página 283.

• Hablen de las diferentes formas de las nubes en el cielo. ¿Qué te recuerdan?

• Ayuden al niño a encontrar consonantes de sonido dígrafo en el poema, tales como: **white**, **sheep**, **when** y **where**. Después encuentren las palabras que riman. (hill/still, slow/go)

P R O J E C T

With your child, read and answer these questions about weather. **Wh**at is the weather like **wh**ere you live? Can you **th**ink of the sound that **th**under makes? Can you find a **sh**adow during a rain **sh**ower? If you had the **ch**ance, how would you **ch**ange the weather?

P R O Y E C T O

Haga las siguientes preguntas sobre el tiempo al niño. ¿Cómo es el tiempo en el lugar donde vives? ¿Puedes imaginar el ruido que hace un trueno? ¿Puedes ver una sombra durante un aguacero? Si tienes la oportunidad ¿cómo puedes cambiar el tiempo?

Th

Thunder starts with the sound of the consonant digraph **th.** Listen for the sound of **th** in the rhyme.

Think about thick clouds,
Think about thunder.
Think of some big things,
You can hide under.

Circle the picture if its name begins with the sound of **th.**

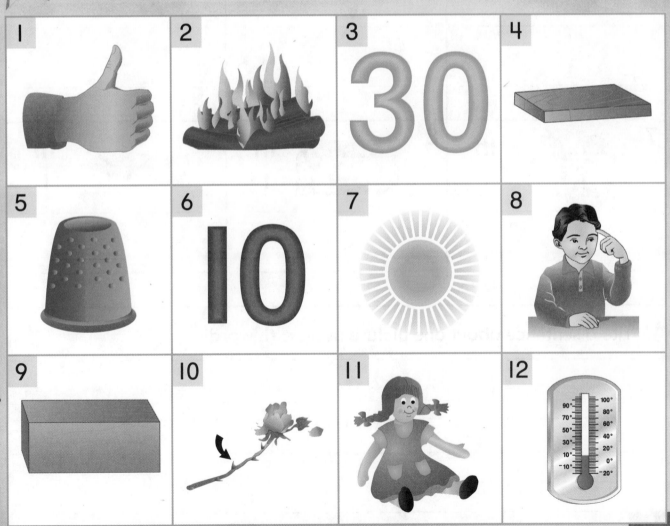

1	2	3	4
5	6	7	8
9	10	11	12

think	tape	thirty	tube	thorn
thumb	top	thick	ten	

1 th t

_____
- - - - - - - - -
_____

2 th t

_____
- - - - - - - - -
_____

3 **10** th t

_____
- - - - - - - - -
_____

4 th t

_____
- - - - - - - - -
_____

5 th t

_____
- - - - - - - - -
_____

6 th t

_____
- - - - - - - - -
_____

7 **30** th t

_____
- - - - - - - - -
_____

8 th t

_____
- - - - - - - - -
_____

9 th t

_____
- - - - - - - - -
_____

Write a sentence about one picture using a **th** word.

_____
- -
_____
- -
_____

sh

Shovel starts with the sound of the consonant digraph **sh.**
Listen for the sound of **sh** in the rhyme.

The sun is shining.
Shout hooray!
Grab a shovel.
Be on your way.

Say the name of each picture. Circle the letters that stand for the beginning sound. Then circle the picture if its name begins with **sh.**

1	2	3	4
sh th	sh th	sh th	sh th

5	6	7	8
sh th	sh th	sh th	sh th

9	10	11	12
sh th	sh th	sh th	sh th

Say the name of each picture. Circle the name and print it. In the last box, draw a picture of a word that begins with **sh.** Print the word.

1 seed sad shed	2 shave save vase	3 hips safe shapes
4 shop stop drop	5 hurt sort shirt	6 gift shelf soft
7 lake shake snake	8 ship hip sip	9

Write a sentence about one picture using an **sh** word.

LESSON 151: Writing Consonant Digraph **sh**

Read aloud all of the words. Have your child say "Shhh!" after each word that begins with the **sh** sound.

White starts with the sound of the consonant digraph **wh.**
Listen for the sound of **wh** in the rhyme.

Where did it come from?
When will it go?
This white whirly fog,
Does anyone know?

Circle the picture if its name begins with the sound of **wh.**

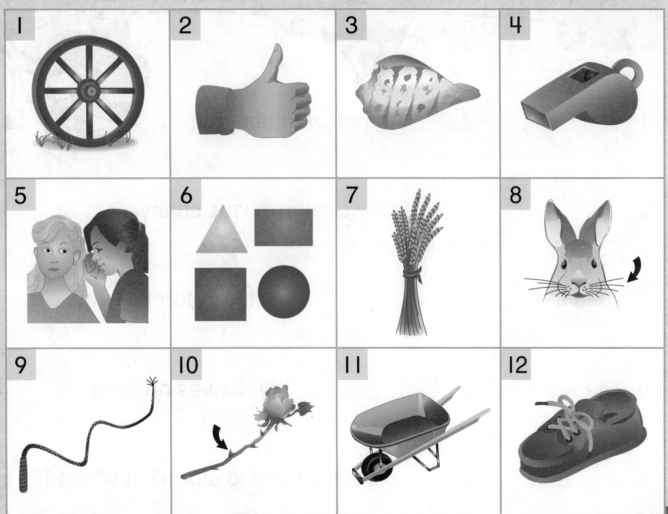

1	2	3	4

5	6	7	8

9	10	11	12

Use a **wh** word from the box to complete each sentence. Print the word on the line. Then read the sentences to a partner.

white	What	whipped	When	Why

1. "_____ a bad weather day!"

2. _____ I woke up, it was sunny.

3. Then the _____ clouds turned gray.

4. The wind _____ the leaves around.

5. "_____ does it have to storm?" I whined.

Take turns with your child asking each other questions that begin with **What, When,** and **Why.**

Chilly starts with the sound of the consonant digraph **ch.**
Listen for the sound of **ch** in the rhyme.

The air is so chilly,
It makes my teeth chatter.
But weather keeps changing,
So what does it matter?

Circle the picture if its name begins with the sound of **ch.**

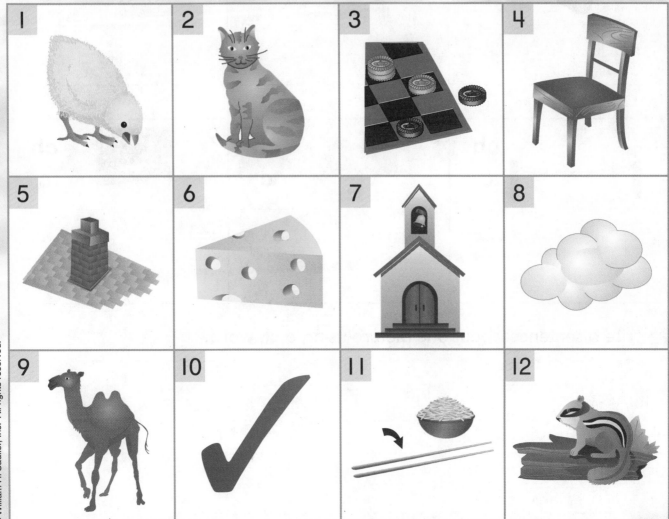

chain	cap	cheek	chin	chop
chalk	coat	chick	cub	

1
ch
c
_____

2
ch
c
_____

3
ch
c
_____

4
ch
c
_____

5
ch
c
_____

6
ch
c
_____

7
ch
c
_____

8
ch
c
_____

9
ch
c
_____

Write a sentence about one picture using a **ch** word.

_____

_____

_____

Knit starts with the sound of the consonant digraph **kn**. The **k** is silent. Listen for the sound made by **kn** in the rhyme.

Mittens warm my knuckles.
Wool pants warm my knees.
I know I should wear a cap.
Will you knit one, please?

Say the name of each picture. Circle **kn** or **k** for each beginning sound. Then circle the picture if its name begins with **kn**.

1	2	3
kn **k**	**kn** **k**	**kn** **k**

4	5	6
kn **k**	**kn** **k**	**kn** **k**

7	8	9
kn **k**	**kn** **k**	**kn** **k**

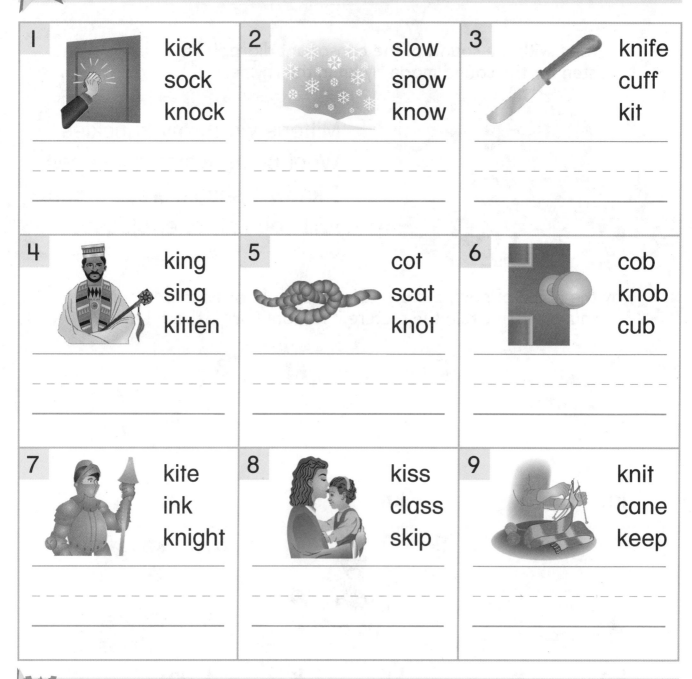

1. kick
   sock
   knock

2. slow
   snow
   know

3. knife
   cuff
   kit

4. king
   sing
   kitten

5. cot
   scat
   knot

6. cob
   knob
   cub

7. kite
   ink
   knight

8. kiss
   class
   skip

9. knit
   cane
   keep

Write a sentence about one of the pictures using a **kn** word.

LESSON 154: Writing Consonant Digraph **kn**

Play "I Know a Word." Take turns with your child naming words that begin with **kn**.

Spell, Write and Tell

Say, spell, and talk about each word in the box.
Then print each word under the digraph in its name.

thing
sheep
white
chain
knob
thin
she
know
think
where
chin
shapes

th
1 _____
2 _____
3 _____

sh
4 _____
5 _____
6 _____

wh
7 _____
8 _____

ch
9 _____
10 _____

kn
11 _____
12 _____

Pretend you are the pilot of a plane. Write about one of your trips in your pilot's log. Use one or more of your spelling words. Then tell about what you wrote.

thing

sheep

white

chain

knob

thin

she

know

think

where

chin

shapes

Date: _____

_____
_____
_____
_____
_____
_____
_____
_____
_____
_____
_____

LESSON 155: Connecting Spelling, Writing, and Speaking

Sit with your child and pretend you are taking a plane ride together. Tell each other what you see.

Read the riddles. Print the answers on the lines. The picture clues will help you. Then circle the words with consonant digraphs.

1. I grow on a tree.
   I am a fruit.

   I am a _____.

2. I swim in the sea,
   but I am not a shark.

   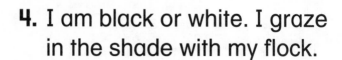

   I am a _____.

3. I may prick you when
   you pick a rose.

   I am a _____.

4. I am black or white. I graze
   in the shade with my flock.

   I am a _____.

5. Open the door with me.
   Then use me to shut it.

   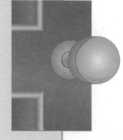

   I am a _____.

Write about and draw a picture of each day's weather. Circle any consonant digraphs you use.

Yesterday it was

_____

- - - - - - - - - - - - - -

_____

- - - - - - - - - - - - - -

_____

Today it is

_____

- - - - - - - - - - - - - -

_____

_____

- - - - - - - - - - - - - -

_____

I think tomorrow will be

_____

- - - - - - - - - - - - - -

_____

_____

- - - - - - - - - - - - - -

_____

LESSON 156: Writing Words with Consonant Digraphs

Watch a television weather report with your child. Listen for words he or she wrote on this page.

Look and Learn

Listen as the page is read aloud. Look at the pictures. Then talk about what you see.

You know there are many kinds of clouds. They come in different shapes and colors.

Cumulus clouds are white and fluffy. You see them when the sun shines. Cirrus clouds look like feathers. When they are in the sky, the weather may change soon. A layer of stratus clouds can cover the sky. Stratus clouds may be gray. They often bring rain.

When you go outside, look up. What are clouds telling you about the weather?

Cumulus Clouds

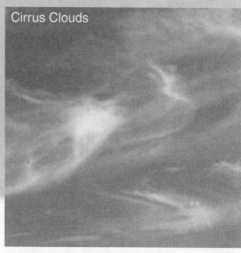
Cirrus Clouds

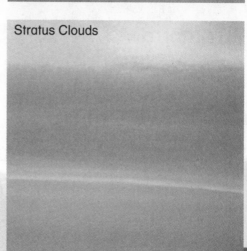
Stratus Clouds

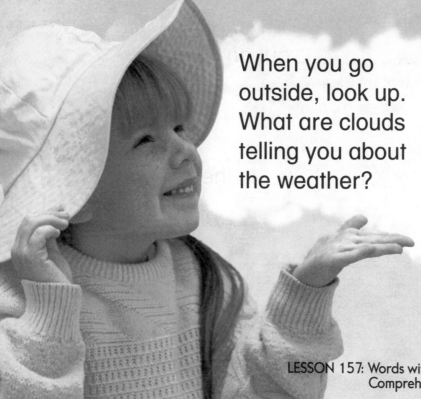

LESSON 157: Words with Consonant Digraphs in Context
Comprehension: Recognizing Facts

299

The words in the box are often used in sentences. Use one of the words to complete each sentence. Then practice reading the sentences aloud.

come	find	open	out	want	We

1. I _____ to plan a 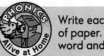 .

2. Dad and Gran will _____ , too.

3. _____ want to see if it will rain.

4. Gran can _____ out on ▢ .

5. Dad can find _____ in the 📰 .

6. I can _____ the ▢ to find out.

PHONICS Alive at Home

Write each word in the box on a piece of paper. Ask your child to read each word and use it in a sentence.

 **Check-Up**

Say the name of each picture. Fill in the circle next to the letters that stand for the beginning digraph.

1		2		3	
	○ **kn** ○ **sh** ○ **th**		○ **ch** ○ **sh** ○ **wh**		○ **th** ○ **ch** ○ **wh**

4		5		6	
	○ **kn** ○ **sh** ○ **ch**	**30**	○ **th** ○ **kn** ○ **sh**		○ **wh** ○ **ch** ○ **kn**

7		8		9	
	○ **ch** ○ **th** ○ **wh**		○ **sh** ○ **kn** ○ **ch**		○ **th** ○ **ch** ○ **wh**

10		11		12	
	○ **ch** ○ **sh** ○ **th**		○ **sh** ○ **wh** ○ **kn**		○ **kn** ○ **th** ○ **ch**

13		14		15	
	○ **ch** ○ **sh** ○ **th**		○ **sh** ○ **th** ○ **kn**		○ **th** ○ **wh** ○ **sh**

 **Check-Up** Say the name of each picture. Find the letters in the box that stand for the missing digraph. Then print the letters on the lines.

th	sh	wh	ch	kn

1 ___ell

2 ___ip

3 ___ick

4 ___op

5 ___ot

6 ___eel

7 ___it

8 ___irt

9 ___ink

10 ___eat

11 ___eese

12 ___ave

LESSON 159: Assessing Consonant Digraphs

Review this Check-Up with your child.

TOMMY

I put a seed into the ground
And said, "I'll watch it grow."
I watered it and cared for it
As well as I could know.

One day I walked in my back yard
And oh, what did I see!
My seed had popped itself right out,
Without consulting me.

Gwendolyn Brooks

Critical Thinking

What would you do to help seeds grow?
What kind of seeds grow into big plants?

Name _____

Dear Family,

As your child progresses through this unit, you can help phonics come alive at home. Your child will learn about things that grow, as well as words that "grow" from other words—compound words, contractions, and words with endings.

● Help your child read the words below.

Apreciada Familia:

A medida que los niños avanzan en esta unidad ustedes pueden revivir los fonemas en la casa. Los niños aprenderán sobre el crecimiento de las cosas y también sobre palabras que "crecen", palabras compuestas, contracciones y terminaciones.

● Ayuden al niño a leer estas palabras.

Compound Word Palabra compuesta	Contraction Contracción	Ending s Terminación s	Ending ing Terminación ing	Ending ed Terminación ed
sunflower	I'll	sees	growing	planted

● Read the poem "Tommy" on the reverse side of this page.

● Talk about things that grow, such as **flowers, kittens,** and, of course, **children.**

● Help your child find compound words in the poem (itself, without), the contraction (I'll), and words with endings (watered, cared, walked, popped, consulting).

● Then make a list of words that rhyme with **grow.** (bow/go/hoe/mow/know/row/sow/toe)

● Lean el poema "Tommy" en la página 303.

● Hablen de las cosas que crecen como las **flores,** y por supuesto, **los niños.**

● Ayuden a su niño a encontrar palabras compuestas en el poema (itself, without) la contracción (I'll) y palabras con terminación (watered, cared, walked, popped, consulting).

● Después hagan una lista de palabras que riman con **grow.** (bow/go/hoe/mow/know/row/sow/toe)

PROJECT

Draw a flower on paper and print **ing** in the center. Help your child make the flower "grow" by printing words with that ending in the petals. Draw another flower using the ending **s.** Use the words in sentences.

PROYECTO

Dibujen una flor y escriban **ing** en el centro. Ayuden a su hijo a hacer "crecer" la flor escribiendo palabras con esa terminación en los pétalos. Dibujen otra flor usando la terminación **s.** Usen las palabras en oraciones.

A compound word is a word made from two or more shorter words. Basketball is a compound word. Listen and look for compound words in the rhyme.

I crawled in my playpen,
When I was small.
Now I climb to the treetops
And play basketball.

P ut two words together to make a compound word. Print the compound word on the line.

1		sun + flower = _____
2		rain + coat = _____
3		wheel + chair = _____
4		wish + bone = _____
5		butter + fly = _____

Say the name of each picture with a partner. Find a word in Box 1 and join it with a word in Box 2 to name the picture. Print the word on the line.

Box 1			Box 2		
pop	rain	mail	chair	pack	lace
shoe	wheel	back	corn	coat	box

1

mailbox

2

3

4

5

6

LESSON 161: Writing Compound Words

With your child, see how many compound words you can make using **man, snow, ball, foot,** and **base.**

A contraction is a short way of writing two words as one. One or more letters are left out. An apostrophe (') shows where the letters were. **Isn't** is a contraction. Look and listen for contractions in the rhyme.

Isn't that a flower bud?
Didn't that baby bird sing?
Everything is growing now.
Can't you tell—it's spring!

C olor each leaf if the contraction stands for the other two words below it.

I am = I'm	she is = she's	we are = we're
	he is = he's	you are = you're
	it is = it's	they are = they're

1	2	3
I'm I am	she's she had	you're you are

4	5	6
it's it is	he's he is	we're I was

7	8	9
they're they are	we're we are	she's she is

Contractions can be made with **will** and **not**.
Read the words on the flower petals. Color
the petals with a contraction that is made
from the word in the center of each flower.

he + will =
he'll

is + not =
isn't

I will = I'll   we will = we'll   is not = isn't
he will = he'll   you will = you'll   do not = don't
she will = she'll   they will = they'll   does not = doesn't
it will = it'll   are not = aren't

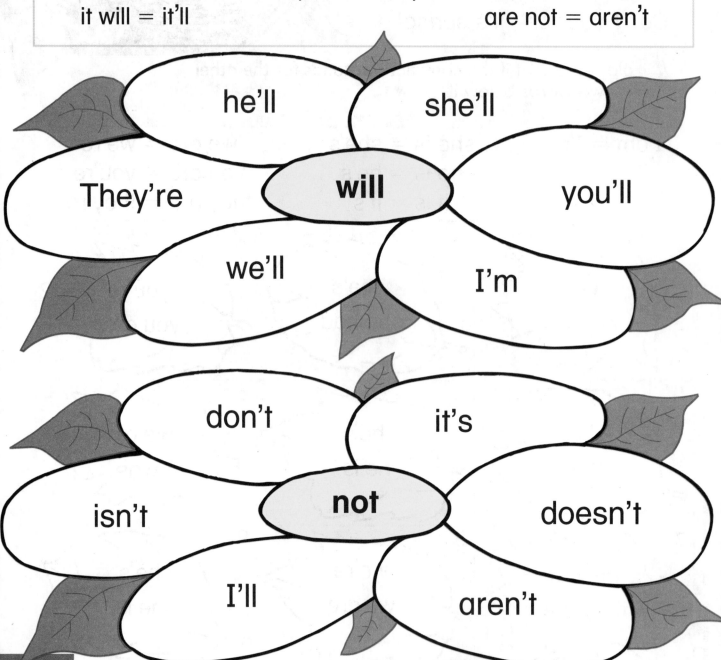

he'll   she'll

They're   **will**   you'll

we'll   I'm

don't   it's

isn't   **not**   doesn't

I'll   aren't

Ask your child to read each contraction
and name the two words from which
it is made.

Spell, Write, and Tell Say, spell, and talk about each word in the box.
Then print each word under the correct heading.

| I'm |
| she's |
| they're |
| doesn't |
| don't |
| they'll |
| it'll |
| we're |
| we'll |
| he's |
| you're |
| isn't |

Contraction with *am*

1 _____

Contractions with *is*

2 _____

3 _____

Contractions with *are*

4 _____

5 _____

6 _____

Contractions with *will*

7 _____

8 _____

9 _____

Contractions with *not*

10 _____

11 _____

12 _____

Spell, Write, and Tell

Write down some things you and your family are planning to do this summer. Use one or more of your spelling words. Then tell about what you wrote.

I'm	they're	don't	it'll	we'll	you're
she's	doesn't	they'll	we're	he's	isn't

My Summer Plans

LESSON 163: Connecting Spelling, Writing, and Speaking

Ask your child to draw a picture showing one of the family activities he or she wrote about.

Thinks was made by adding **s** to the end of the base word **think**. Listen and look for words that end in **s** in the rhyme.

"Oh no, rain!" Ann thinks.
But the oak tree smiles.
It drinks and drinks.

Add **s** to the base word in the box. Print the new word on the line.

#			
1		Dad _____ in the yard.	dig
2		Adam _____ the seeds.	plant
3		Tasha _____ the plants.	water
4		The garden _____ .	grow
5		Gram _____ the peas.	pick

Rowing and **rowed** were made by adding **ing** and **ed** to the end of the base word **row**. Listen and look for words that end in **ing** or **ed** in the rhyme.

Last year grandpa rowed,
But now I am rowing.
I'm learning new things
Because I am growing.

Look at each picture and read the base word in Column 1. Add **ing** to the base word in Column 2. Add **ed** to the base word in Column 3.

Column 1	Column 2	Column 3
Base Word	**+ ing**	**+ ed**
1 mix	mixing	mixed
2 kick		
3 yell		
4 crawl		

LESSON 164: Recognizing Inflectional Endings **ing** and **ed**

Help your child add **ing** and **ed** to **walk**, **look**, and **play.** Then make up sentences for the new words.

Work Together

Take turns reading the sentences with a partner. Find the ending of the word in dark type and circle it. Then print the base word on the line.

1. The farmer is **p l a n t (i n g)** a new crop.

plant

2. The baby duck **q u a c k e d**.

3. The puppy **p l a y s** with me.

4. Keesha **s p i l l e d** the bag of seeds.

5. The boat is **s a i l i n g** on the lake.

Listen as the poem is read aloud. Draw a line under the words that end with **ing** and **ed.** Then write a complete sentence to answer each question.

Living Things Grow

At first, baby Toyo crawled,
But soon he could walk.
He was playing and laughing
And learning to talk.

All living things grow up,
Not just me and you.
Seeds, trees, birds, and pups—
They're all growing, too.

I. How can you tell that something is growing up?

_____

_____

_____

_____

2. What things have you learned since you were a baby?

_____

_____

_____

_____

LESSON 165: Words with Inflectional Endings **ing** and **ed** in Context
Comprehension: Making Generalizations

Tell your child what he or she was like as a baby. Talk about how your child has grown.

Look and Learn

Listen as the page is read aloud.
Look at the pictures. Then
talk about what you see.

All living things grow.
Sunflowers grow.
So do animals such as tigers.
You're growing, too. Aren't you?

Try matching the young plants
and animals to the older ones.
How are they the same?
How are they different?
How do they change as they grow?

Look at a baby picture of yourself.
Don't you look different now?
How have you changed?

LESSON 166: Compound Words, Contractions, and Words with Endings in Context
Comprehension: Comparing and Contrasting

315

Ready to Read

The words in the box are often used in sentences. Use one of the words to complete each sentence. Then practice reading the sentences aloud.

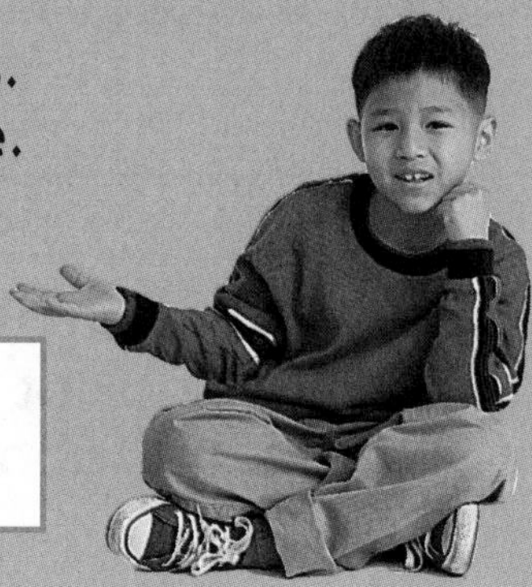

ask	going	he	just	play	up

1. "Tim can not walk ________ the ," said Tom.

2. "Tim can not ________ for help yet," said Mom.

3. "Tim is ________ a ," said Mom.

4. "Will Tim ________  with me?" asked Tom.

5. "Will ________ ride to the  with me?" asked Tom.

6. "Tim is ________ to need you, Tom!" said Mom.

PHONICS Alive at Home

Together with your child, use the words in the box to make up sentences about the baby in the story.

Make a compound word by drawing a line from the first word in the box to another word in the box. Print the compound word on the line.

1		
rain	coat wish sun	

2		
pop	sticks corn robin	

3		
mail	pen box sail	

4		
shoe	pack ball lace	

5		
wish	bone nut wind	

6		
wheel	news chair base	

7		
back	plane chair pack	

8		
butter	fly ball wheel	

 **Check-Up** Circle the contraction that stands for the underlined words.

1 she is	she'll she's isn't	7 do not	don't doesn't aren't	13 you are	you'll they'll you're
2 I will	we'll I'll I'm	8 it is	it's it'll we'll	14 he will	we're he's he'll
3 they will	they'll they're I'll	9 are not	isn't it'll aren't	15 you will	you're you'll he'll
4 they are	aren't they'll they're	10 I am	I'll I'm it's	16 she will	she'll she's he'll
5 is not	it's isn't I'll	11 we will	we'll we're they'll	17 does not	don't aren't doesn't
6 it will	it'll it's I'll	12 he is	he'll he's she's	18 we are	we'll you're we're

Review this Check-Up with your child.

Read each sentence. Circle the word that completes each sentence. Then print the word on the line.

1 It is _____ on my hat!	rain rained raining
2 I _____ for Sam to come home.	yells yelled yelling
3 The man _____ here for the bus.	wait waits waiting
4 Dad is _____ the grass.	mows mowed mowing
5 Jim _____ Sue bake a cake.	help helped helping
6 That boat _____ on the lake.	sail sails sailing

Read each sentence. Circle the word that completes each sentence. Then print the word on the line.

I	The dog is _____ up on me.	jumps jumped jumping
2	I _____ to play with the cat.	wants wanted wanting
3	Dad _____ the flute.	play plays playing
4	I am _____ you a big box.	mail mailed mailing
5	Jill _____ home with Tom.	walk walks walking
6	Mom _____ the pot to the top.	fill filled filling

STUDENT SKILLS
ASSESSMENT CHECKLIST

☑ Assessed ☒ Retaught ■ Mastered

Unit 1 **Phonemic Awareness and Auditory Discrimination**
- ❑ Phonemic Awareness: Rhyming Sounds
- ❑ Phonemic Awareness: Initial Sounds

Unit 2 **Consonant Sounds**
- ❑ Initial Consonant **f**
- ❑ Initial Consonant **m**
- ❑ Initial Consonant **s**
- ❑ Final Consonants **f, ff, m, s, ss**
- ❑ Initial Consonant **t**
- ❑ Initial Consonant **h**
- ❑ Initial Consonant **b**
- ❑ Final Consonants **t, tt, b**
- ❑ Consonants **f, m, s, t, h, b**
- ❑ Initial Consonant **l**
- ❑ Initial Consonant **d**
- ❑ Initial Consonant **c**
- ❑ Final Consonants **l, ll, d, dd**
- ❑ Initial Consonant **n**
- ❑ Initial Consonant **g**
- ❑ Initial Consonant **w**
- ❑ Final Consonants **n, g, gg**
- ❑ Consonants **l, d, c, n, g, w**
- ❑ Initial Consonant **p**
- ❑ Initial Consonant **r**
- ❑ Initial Consonant **k**
- ❑ Final Consonants **p, r, k**
- ❑ Initial Consonant **j**
- ❑ Initial Consonant **q(u)**
- ❑ Initial Consonant **v**

Teacher Comments

- ❑ Final Consonant **v**
- ❑ Initial Consonants **y** and **z**
- ❑ Final Consonants **x** and **zz**
- ❑ Consonants **p, r, k, s, q(u), v, x, y, z**
- ❑ Double Final Consonants **ff, ss, tt, ll, dd, gg, zz**
- ❑ Medial Consonants
- ❑ Initial, Medial, Final Consonants
- ❑ High-Frequency Words **by, funny, let, ride, stop, walk**

Unit 3 Short Vowels

- ❑ Short Vowel **a**
- ❑ Short Vowel **i**
- ❑ Short Vowel **o**
- ❑ Short Vowel **u**
- ❑ Short Vowel **e**
- ❑ High-Frequency Words **and, help, it, no, see, will**

Unit 4 Long Vowels

- ❑ Long Vowel **a**
- ❑ Long Vowel **i**
- ❑ Long Vowel **o**
- ❑ Long Vowel **u**
- ❑ Long Vowel **e**
- ❑ Final **y** as a Vowel
- ❑ High-Frequency Words **down, here, little, please, put, said**

Unit 5 Consonant Blends

- ❑ **L** Blends
- ❑ **R** Blends
- ❑ **S** Blends
- ❑ Final Consonant Blends
- ❑ High-Frequency Words **again, ate, big, look, to, yellow**

Unit 6 Consonant Digraphs

- ❑ Consonant Digraph **th**
- ❑ Consonant Digraph **sh**
- ❑ Consonant Digraph **wh**
- ❑ Consonant Digraph **ch**
- ❑ Consonant Digraph **kn**
- ❑ High-Frequency Words **come, find, open, out, want, we**

Unit 7 Word Structure

- ❑ Compound Words
- ❑ Contractions
- ❑ Inflectional Endings **s, ing, ed**
- ❑ High-Frequency Words **ask, going, he, just, play, up**

Name _____

Good Books

— Fold —

Reading at Home: Read the book with your child. Help your child identify the rhyming words, such as **sea** and **free**. Then talk about all of the different places shown in the story.

3

— Fold —

on the ranch or in the sea.

Draw a picture of a book
you would like to share.

8 ✂

Fun adventures, silly rhymes!

6   ✂

Directions: Cut and fold the book.

Unit 1 Take-Home Book
Comprehension: Identifying the Setting

323

I'm never bored. I feel so free

Fold

4

I have good times. I make new friends.

Fold

I never want the books to end.

5

Good books, good times!

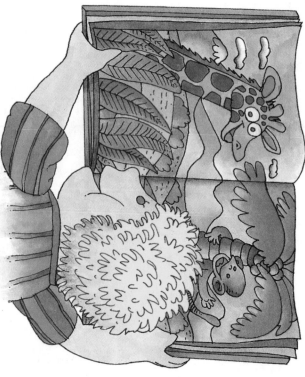

Unit 1 Take-Home Book
Comprehension: Identifying the Setting

Name _____

I LOVE PARADES

1

Fold

3

with funny clowns,

Fold

and me!
Draw a picture to show
what you do in the parade.

8

razzle-dazzle
floats that ride by,

6

Directions: Cut and fold the book.

Unit 2 Take-Home Book
Comprehension: Sequencing

325

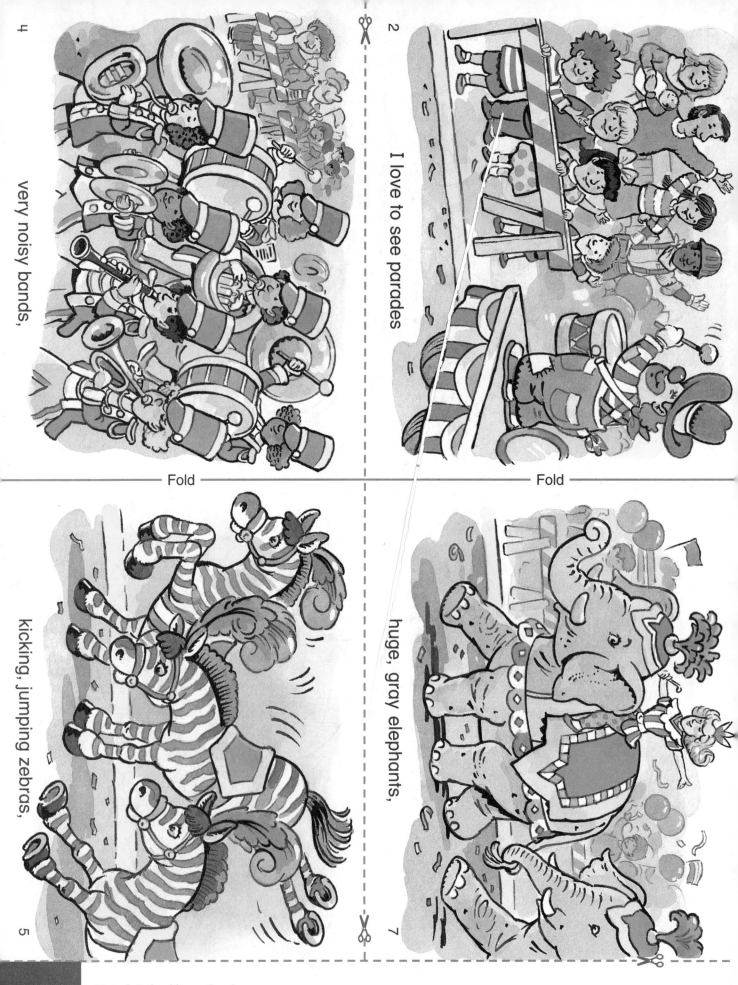

4

very noisy bands,

2

I love to see parades

Fold

Fold

huge, gray elephants,

kicking, jumping zebras,

5

7

Name _____

Is It a Bug?

— Fold —

1

✂

3

Is a lion a bug?

An ant lion is.

— Fold —

It will grow up to be a moth.

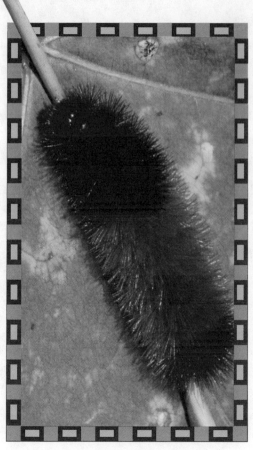

A lion, a fish, and a bear—all are bugs you see!
Were you surprised?

8

✂

A silverfish bends like a fish in a pond.
It snacks on books or rugs.

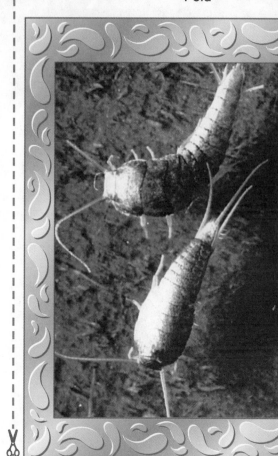

6

Directions: Cut and fold the book.

Unit 3 Take-Home Book
Comprehension: Setting a Purpose for Reading

327

4

An ant lion digs a pit to make a trap. It gobbles up other bugs that drop in.

What is a bug?

I bet you'll be surprised.

Fold

Is a fish a bug?

A silverfish is.

5

Fold

Is a bear a bug?

A woolly bear is.

7

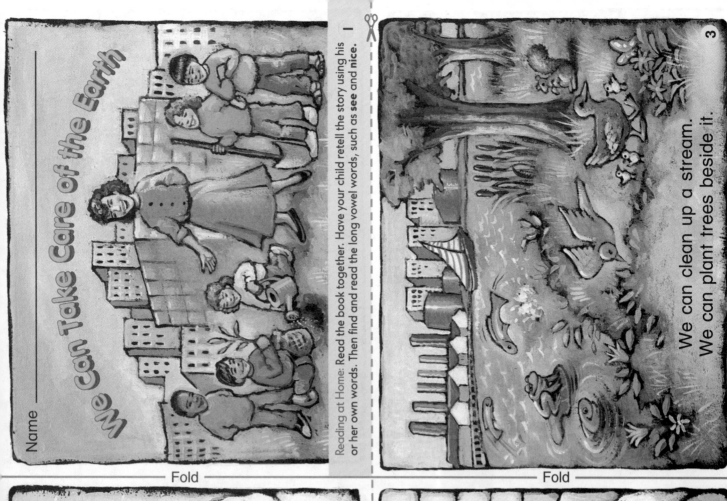

Name _____

We Can Take Care of the Earth

Reading at Home: Read the book together. Have your child retell the story using his or her own words. Then find and read the long vowel words, such as **see** and **nice**.

Fold

1

3

Fold

We can clean up a stream.
We can plant trees beside it.

President of the United States
The White House
Washington, DC 20502

We can learn the rules and tell what we know. Please write to someone who can help.

8

We can turn off the water while we brush our teeth.

6

Directions: Cut and fold the book.

Unit 4 Take-Home Book
Comprehension: Retelling a Story

4

We can try to save paper.
We can take bags to the grocery store.

Fold

2

See how the earth looks.
It doesn't look nice.
What can we do?

Fold

5

We can be sure to turn off
the lights when we go outside.

7

RECYCLING SALE

We can recycle used toys.
We can put them on sale.

Making Sense

Name _____

Fold

Fold

Reading at Home: Read the book together. As you answer the questions, decide which answers are facts and which are opinions. Then find the pictures that have blends in their names, such as **plane** and **grapes**.

1

What sounds loud?

3

What smells good?

It looks _____

It feels _____

It is a _____

8

6

Directions: Cut and fold the book.

Unit 5 Take-Home Book
Comprehension: Distinguishing Fact/Opinion

331

4

What tastes best to you?

2

What looks blue?

Fold

Fold

What feels soft?

Look! What is this?
Print your guess on the next page.

5

7

Unit 5 Take-Home Book
Comprehension: Distinguishing Fact/Opinion

WEATHER CHANGES

1

Fold

Fold

Weather changes.
Storms dash by.
Soon it should be
Warm and dry.

Thunder's knocking.
Crash and flash!
Rain is swishing.
Splish! Splash!

8

Directions: Cut and fold the book.

Unit 6 Take-Home Book
Comprehension: Drawing Conclusions

33

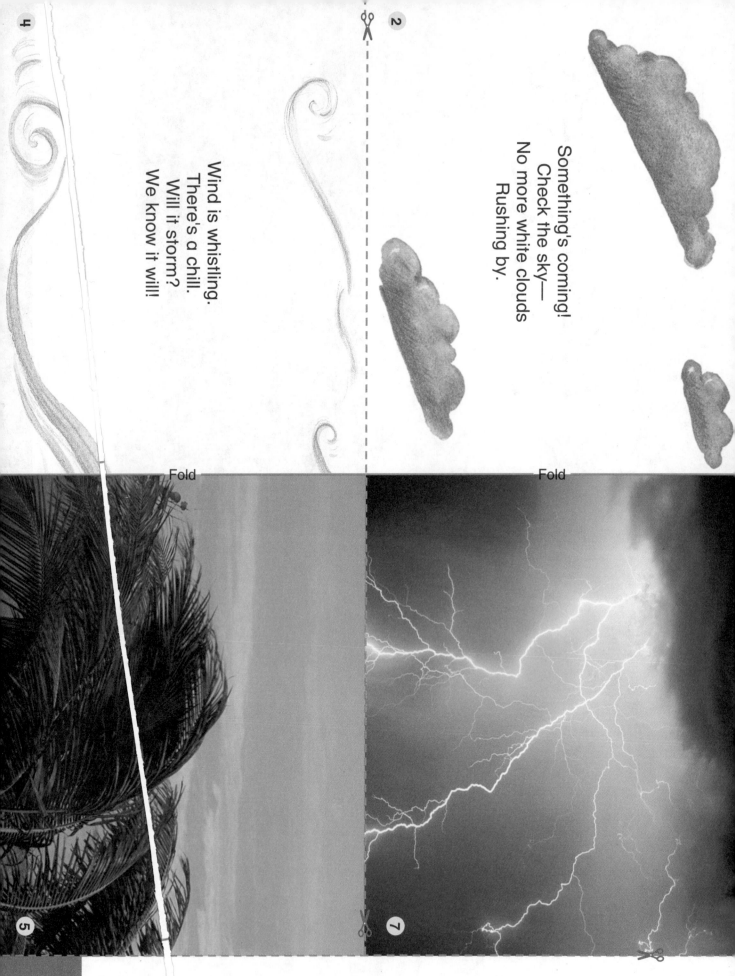

4

Something's coming!
Check the sky—
No more white clouds
Rushing by.

Wind is whistling.
There's a chill.
Will it storm?
We know it will!

Fold

Fold

5

7

Unit 6 Take-Home Book
Comprehension: Drawing Conclusions

Growing Up

Name _____

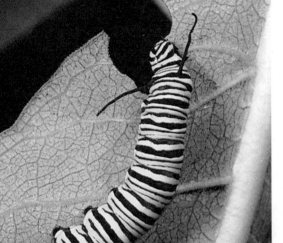

Fold

1

✂

It starts eating and eating.

3

Fold

Growing up looks pretty good, don't you think?

8

✂

Doesn't the bug's new home look funny?

6

Directions: Cut and fold the book.

Unit 7 Take-Home Book
Comprehension: Comparing and Contrasting

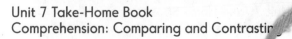

335

Someday this little bug is going to be a butterfly.

It grows bigger every day.

Fold

Fold

Then it hangs upside down.

Soon the butterfly comes out.

Unit 7 Take-Home Book
Comprehension: Comparing and Contrasting